Seasoning YOUR WORDS

Updated & Revised

Nancy Eichman

Seasoning
YOUR
WORDS

God's Recipe for
Controlling Your Tongue

GOSPEL
ADVOCATE
A TRUSTED NAME SINCE 1855

Published by Gospel Advocate Co.
1006 Elm Hill Pike, Nashville, TN 37210
www.gospeladvocate.com

ISBN: 978-0-89225-463-7

DEDICATION

To our children,
John and Amy, with much love.

Also by Nancy Eichman

God's Makeover Plan

Keeping Your Balance

Conquering Your Giants

The Road to Forgiveness

Getting Along

Beyond the Masquerade

What's On the
MENU?

Apple Pie
& Many Thanks to ...

Jane McWhorter, for continued encouragement

Joy Miller, for her helpful editorial comments

George and Ellen Welker, for their painstaking proofreading

Henry Terrill and Laurie Fox of the library staff
at Harding University for their help in research

Cecil and Milbra Chaffin, my parents, for
their stalwart spiritual support

Phil, my husband, for his patient editorial
and moral support

Phil, Amy and John, my family, for giving me
the time to write

Just a Few Words

*W*ho do you think talks more – men or women?

For centuries, women have been stereotyped as constant chatterboxes, gabbing all the time. Take this quip for instance, "God made man before He made woman because He wanted to have a little talk with him without interruption." Another wit has noted, "Women live longer than men because they need time to finish all they started to say." It is generally true that women express themselves more often through words and are more verbal with their feelings than men. Someone once said that the average woman talks 50 percent more than her husband listens. Let's face it – women like to talk.

However, a 2014 study has found that many men like to talk a lot too. Northeastern University researchers discovered that men and women each could talk a blue streak. It just depends on the setting. They observed that women were more comfortable conversing longer in smaller groups while men did most of the talking in groups of six or more.

Although there will still be people who think women trump men in word count, we do know that none of us are immune to the faults of the tongue. Controlling the tongue is a constant challenge for any Christian.

Some people may downplay the effect of their words by saying, "They're only words" or "Sticks and stones may break my bones, but words will never hurt me." But words are powerful. Like a forest fire raging out of control, ill-chosen words can ravage and sear the heart. Appropriate, timely words can soothe the deep burning pains of the soul.

By appreciating the immense power of the negative and the positive uses of the tongue, we can be more effective in God's kingdom. That is my prayer for everyone who uses this study.

Each chapter is introduced by "Food for Thought," quotes about the tongue from various sources. Selected scriptures pertinent to the subject in the chapter are included in "Feeding on God's Word." "Think About It" provides questions that delve further into each chapter's topic and may be used for class discussion or personal study.

She Couldn't
Stop

Sally had a great big mouth,
And she was quick to use it.
But all the people in our town
Just wished that she would lose it!

For no one, whether great or small,
Was safe from Sally's mouth.
What juicy news her nose sniffed out
Her tongue spread north to south.

Then one day Sally lost her teeth,
And dentures were her lot.
We thought that these would slow her tongue,
But it just faster got.

Her mouth kept flying till her death.
Her grave has flowers growing.
But Sally dear is with us still —
Her choppers still are going!

Food
For Thought

"Words are like medicine: they should be measured
with care, for an overdose may hurt."

(Jewish proverb)

"Every time you speak, your mind is on parade."

(Unknown)

"When your thoughts run riot your tongue
is apt to join the crowd."

(Unknown)

Feed on God's Word

Look up these scriptures, and put in
your own words what they mean.

Psalm 19:14

_____
_____
_____

Proverbs 12:13

_____
_____
_____

Proverbs 15:28

_____
_____
_____

Proverbs 16:23

_____
_____
_____

Matthew 15:17-20

_____
_____
_____

How Tasteful Are Your Words?

"For the ear tests words as the tongue tastes food.
Let us discern for ourselves what is right;
let us learn together what is good"
(Job 34:3-4).

*W*ords. We have them; we cut them short; we mince them; we play on them; we hang on to them; we even eat them.

Paul wrote about doing something else with words – seasoning them. "Let your conversation be always full of grace, seasoned with salt, so that you may know how to answer everyone" (Colossians 4:6). This is the only time "seasoned with salt" is used in the Bible. What meaning did this expression have for Paul and the readers of his epistle?

Importance of Salt

Centuries before Paul's time, salt was the most commonly used seasoning. Job asked, "Is tasteless food eaten without salt?" (Job 6:6). Salt also was used in religious rites and ceremonies.

In Paul's day, salt was such a precious commodity that often it was traded for gold. To buy salt, Roman soldiers were paid an allowance or "salt money" (the Latin *salarium*, from which our word "salary" is derived). The first trade routes traversing Egypt, Greece, Italy and Spain were built for the purpose of transporting salt.

Salt has received bad publicity today because of its excessive use, but salt is a necessity for living things. Humans and animals always have had a physical need for the sodium and chloride in salt.

Seasoning With Salt

Seeing how valuable and necessary salt was to the people of Paul's day gives us a clearer picture of why he admonished his hearers' speech to be seasoned with salt. Focusing on some attributes of salt, seen in a spiritual sense, should improve the quality of our speech.

Salt saves. Before the invention of refrigeration or the practice of canning, salt was used for preserving fresh meat and fish. Spiritually, if any saving influence is to come through our speech, we must guard our lips carefully. If we utter a smorgasbord of tasteless and rash words with foul expletives, how can we reach people for Christ?

Salt flavors. Someone once said, "Salt is what makes things bad when it isn't in them." Salt can take a bland dish and make it tasty. So it is with our speech. When we belong to Christ, our words can be wholesome and tasteful rather than flat and dull. Interestingly, the word "salt" symbolized the wit and pungency of speech to Greeks and Romans.

Jesus spoke about the danger of losing this positive flavorful influence. "You are the salt of the earth. But if the salt loses its saltiness, how can it be made salty again? It is no longer good for anything, except to be thrown out and trampled by men" (Matthew 5:13).

Salt cleanses. Elisha threw salt into the Jericho spring to cleanse it (2 Kings 2:20-22). The Israelites used salt to bathe newborn babies (Ezekiel 16:4), and this custom continues in some regions of the world today. Our speech needs to be cleansed as well. God cannot be pleased with a dirty mouth.

Salt de-ices. When ice freezes on a road or sidewalk, salt is applied to initiate the melting process. So it is when a hard heart interacts with the melting salt of kind words. No wonder Jesus said, "Salt is good, but if it loses its saltiness, how can you make it salty again? Have salt in yourselves, and be at peace with each other" (Mark 9:50).

Salt operates internally. When salt is mixed into food, we can't see what happens. We just know that food tastes better. The change takes place from the inside. Likewise, our speech must be controlled from within to be effective. From our thoughts flow our words. Someone put it well: "What you say reveals much. What you don't say reveals much more."

From Thoughts to Words

The output from our mouths depends on the input of the thoughts of the heart. Whether we like it or not, we usually don't say something unless it first has been on our minds. An unknown sage wrote, "Be careful of your thoughts; they may break into words at any time." The wise man put it well: "Above all else, guard your heart, for it is the wellspring of life. Put away perversity from your mouth; keep corrupt talk far from your lips" (Proverbs 4:23-24).

Justin Martyr, an early church father, said, "By examining the tongue of a patient, the physician finds out the diseases of the body, and the philosopher the diseases of the mind." What spiritual diseases lurk behind our words? Murmuring words reveal a critical heart. A swearing tongue indicates a sacrilegious heart. Boastful words flow from a proud heart. Gossip springs from a thoughtless heart.

Jesus perceived the evil hearts and resulting bad fruit of the hypocritical Pharisees when He said, "Make a tree good and its fruit will be good, or make a tree bad and its fruit will be bad, for a tree is recognized by its fruit. You brood of vipers, how can you who are evil say anything good? For out of the overflow of the heart the mouth speaks. The good man brings good things out of the good stored up in him, and the evil man brings evil things out of the evil stored up in him" (Matthew 12:33-35).

We may not always speak our minds, but God knows our thoughts. "Before a word is on my tongue you know it completely, O LORD" (Psalm 139:4). We cannot hide our hearts from Him. A foolproof method of keeping our words clean is to be sure our hearts are spotless. We can take Paul's advice: "Finally, brothers, whatever is true, whatever is noble, whatever is right, whatever is pure, whatever is lovely, whatever is admirable – if anything is excellent or praiseworthy – think about such things" (Philippians 4:8).

May we be able to pray like the psalmist, "Though you probe my heart and examine me at night, though you test me, you will find nothing; I have resolved that my mouth will not sin" (Psalm 17:3).

Some words are tasteful, but others leave a disagreeable aftertaste in our mouths. Are we seasoning with salt? How do your words taste today?

Think About It

1. Explain why salt was important in ancient times.

2. Name the good qualities of salt. How do they compare spiritually to the positive use of the tongue?

3. "Words are the guide to acts: the mouth makes the first move" (Leone Da Modena). In the biblical examples below, tell how words eventually led to actions.

   a. Serpent to Adam and Eve (Genesis 3:1-7)

   b. Joseph's brothers to each other (Genesis 37:18-28)

   c. Joshua to the Israelites (Joshua 24:14-27)

   d. John the Baptist to Herodias (Mark 6:17-29)

   e. Peter to the audience on Pentecost (Acts 2:14-41)

4. What did Paul mean by taking "captive every thought to make it obedient to Christ" (2 Corinthians 10:5)? What are some ways we can do this?

5. Can we hide any of our thoughts from God (Hebrews 4:12-13; Psalm 94:11)?

6. Was there a time when you spoke before you thought? What can help us follow James' advice to be "slow to speak" (James 1:19)?

7. Where in the Bible are these expressions, and who said them?

   a. "My words are on the tip of my tongue."

   b. "I have put my words in your mouth."

   c. "You will be protected from the lash of the tongue."

   d. "I will put a muzzle on my mouth."

   e. "Your words are a blustering wind."

   f. "Clap your hand over your mouth."

   g. "His speech is smooth as butter."

8. Who "searches every heart and understands every motive behind the thoughts" (1 Chronicles 28:9)?

9. How do the Lord and man differ in viewing the outward appearance and the heart (1 Samuel 16:7)?

10. Where were the Colossians told to set their hearts and minds to help get rid of sinful speech (Colossians 3:1-10)?

Food For Thought

"Half the world is composed of people who have something to say and can't, and the other half who have nothing to say, and keep on saying it."

(Robert Frost)

"As we must account for every idle word, so we must for every idle silence."

(Benjamin Franklin)

"After all is said and done, more is said than done."

(Unknown)

"Some people speak from experience. Others, from experience, don't speak."

(Unknown)

"Let thy speech be better than silence, or be silent."

(Dionysius of Halicarnassus)

Feed on God's Word

Look up these scriptures, and put in
your own words what they mean.

Psalm 141:3

_____
_____
_____

Proverbs 12:23

_____
_____
_____

Proverbs 16:27

_____
_____
_____

Proverbs 18:13

_____
_____
_____

Matthew 25:11

_____
_____
_____

How Big Was My Mouth?

"Dentopedology is the science of opening your mouth and putting your foot in it. I've been practicing it for years."
(Prince Philip)

The North American Plains Indians had a peculiar method of training their children to keep their mouths shut. When an infant started to cry, its mother covered its mouth with her palm and grasped its nose between her thumb and forefinger. She kept holding until the baby nearly suffocated; then she let go. Again and again this occurred until the little one learned that silence was the best policy.

Although this method seems extreme to us, we wish for an effective way to help our children learn to hold their tongues. They spend about a year or two learning how to talk and a lifetime undoing the damage of their unguarded words. Parents can't wait to hear their child say his or her first word, but after a few weeks they are ready for a reprieve. The child has entered a point of no return when he or she becomes a talker.

Proverbs Fit for a King

King Solomon knew a lot about talkers – he had 700 wives and 300 concubines. Imagine all those words ricocheting off the royal palace walls. I wonder if it sounded like the incessant cackling in a hen house. Perhaps more than once Solomon nodded, said, "Yes, dear," and walked away.

Solomon knew the trouble that people can get into by the misuse of their tongues. This wise king judged cases that involved slanderous, untrue or angry words. His only recorded judgment in the Bible involved a mother who had smothered her newborn accidentally. She lied so that she might take another mother's child for her own (1 Kings 3:16-28).

Solomon's wisdom and experience came together in many of the Proverbs. In that book "words," "lips," "tongue" and "mouth" are mentioned more than 100 times. Solomon must have thought speech to be an important subject. Here is a sampling of some of his wisdom in that book:

> "When words are many, sin is not absent, but he who holds his tongue is wise" (10:19).

> "He who guards his lips guards his life, but he who speaks rashly will come to ruin" (13:3).

> "A man finds joy in giving an apt reply – and how good is a timely word!" (15:23).

> "A man of knowledge uses words with restraint, and a man of understanding is even-tempered. Even a fool is thought wise if he keeps silent, and discerning if he holds his tongue" (17:27-28).

> "The tongue has the power of life and death, and those who love it will eat its fruit" (18:21).

> "He who guards his mouth and his tongue keeps himself from calamity" (21:23).

Unfortunately, people have not heeded Solomon's advice, and they continue to suffer the ill effects of overuse of the mouth, as noted in this poem:

Sportmouthship

Some folks chafe from saddle sores
Or wince from pitcher's wrist.
They groan from the aerobics class
Where their ankles got a twist.
Some folks have tennis elbow or
From jogger's knee they boast,
But running mouth is what some people
Exercise the most!

Mouth Trouble

The Bible contains numerous examples of people whose tongues brought trouble for themselves or other people. Seduced by Satan's devious lie, Adam and Eve were cast out of the Garden of Eden, and sin came into the world (Genesis 3). Near calamity came upon Pharaoh and Abimelech, king of Gerar, when each almost took Sarah as his wife after Abraham's fib (12:10-20; 20). With a deceitful lie, Jacob stole the blessing that belonged to his brother, Esau (27). Jacob's sons caused undue grief to their father when they said Joseph was killed by a wild beast (37:12-36).

Achan lied about the bounty he stole from the ruins of Ai, which caused the loss of the next battle and his life (Joshua 7–8). Doeg's telling King Saul the whereabouts of David caused the death of 85 priests (1 Samuel 22:9-18). Nebuchadnezzar's proud words caused him to live like a wild animal, eating grass in the field (Daniel 4:28-33). Ananias and Sapphira's lie about their gift of money to the church brought them sudden death (Acts 5:1-11).

We wonder, should we speak at all? As Publilius Syrus said in the first century B.C., "I have often regretted my speech, never my silence."

Silence – Not Always Golden

But is it always best to keep quiet? No. If I know that someone has a grudge against me, I should try to clear it up with her (Matthew 5:23-24). I must tell the truth when giving legal testimony (Exodus 23:1-3, 6-7). If someone is being accused falsely, I need to stand up for her (Leviticus 5:1). The same Solomon who wrote about the evils of the wagging tongue also wrote that there was a time for silence and a time for speech (Ecclesiastes 3:7). Our problem is knowing when it is time to speak. As someone once said, "Most of us know how to say nothing; few of us know when."

Some people in the Bible knew when to speak up. Abigail's soothing words averted disaster to herself and her household as she met an angry horde of men and their vengeful commander David (1 Samuel 25:23-34). Jonah's preaching turned around the whole spiritual destiny of the city of Nineveh (Jonah 3:3-10). Daniel prevented death for his friends and himself by speaking with wisdom and tact to Arioch, the commander of the king's guard (Daniel 2:14). Judas and Silas were sent by the Jerusalem apostles and elders "to confirm by word of mouth" what had been written (Acts 15:27). Peter, Paul, Philip and the other apostles used their lips to spread the gospel despite discouragement and persecution.

James and the Untamed Animal

James, in his practical book about Christian living, did not touch lightly on the subject of the tongue. Each chapter in the book contains information about the vices and virtues of speech.

What do horse bits, ship rudders and sparks of fire have in common? James states that they, like the tongue, are small and yet they control much greater things.

A proud stallion is restrained by the pull on the reins connected to the bit in his mouth. A huge ship is maneuvered by its comparatively small rudder. One tiny spark of fire can set thousands of acres of forests ablaze. "The tongue also is a fire, a world of evil among the parts of the body. It corrupts the whole person, sets the whole course of his life on fire, and is itself set on fire by hell" (James 3:6).

Because of the tongue's relatively small size, we often don't realize its Jekyll-and-Hyde potential for evil as well as for good. But James says one little tongue can teach, boast, praise, curse, quarrel, slander, grumble, swear, sing, pray, confess and corrupt the whole person.

In today's world, we can see another example of the Jekyll-and-Hyde potential for evil and good through the use of the tongue. The wide range of social media like Facebook, Twitter, Pinterest, YouTube and other applications provides boundless opportunities to connect with friends, expand our creativity and advertise worthwhile causes, like teaching the gospel and learning new songs through video. However, sometimes things can get ugly. For example, when the "Ice Bucket Challenge" videos went viral on Facebook and YouTube, a call for support for a worthy cause sadly morphed into a chance for some participants to use vulgar language when they were drenched with ice water. The opportunities are there for good. Now if we can only tame our tongues.

Men have traveled to the far reaches of the globe to capture exotic animals and tame them for circuses and fairs. These people often are rewarded for their expense and effort. But the tongue is one of the elusive animals that man has had little success in taming (James 3:8).

We can be thankful that God offers something that greatly aids in the taming process – His wisdom. "If any of you lacks wisdom, he should ask God, who gives generously to all without finding fault, and it will be given to him. … But the wisdom that comes from heaven is first of all pure; then peace-loving, considerate, submissive, full of mercy and good fruit, impartial and sincere" (James 1:5; 3:17). Perhaps we can't tame our tongues, but God can.

Think About It

1. Give some biblical examples – other than those mentioned in this chapter – of people who used their tongues for good or evil.

2. Find other scriptures in Proverbs that pertain to the use of the tongue.

3. Name the item David compared the tongue to in these scriptures:

   Psalm 52:2

   Psalm 57:4

   Psalm 64:3

4. To what did James compare the tongue in James 3:3-8?

5. What things are contrasted in James 3:9-12 to show the good and evil uses of the tongue?

6. What help does God offer us to overcome the vices of the tongue (James 3:17-18)?

7. Instead of boasting and bragging about the future, what should we say (James 4:13-17)?

8. Explain how words can be used to help troubled or sick people (James 5:13-16).

9. Give examples of times when it is wiser to speak up.

10. "A good listener is not only popular everywhere, but after a while he knows something" (Unknown). Explain some other advantages of being a good listener.

Poisonous Words: A Pinch of Poison

"But no man can tame the tongue. It is a restless evil, full of deadly poison" (James 3:8).

I remember a mystery thriller in which the husband murders his wife by poisoning her. She dies immediately, but the husband isn't a suspect because he ate food from the same dish that killed his wife. Upon further investigation, however, it is discovered that the husband slowly had been acclimating his body to increasing doses of the same poison. When he finally carried out the foul scheme on his wife, he suffered no ill effects because he was used to the poison.

Is our speech being sprinkled with little pinches of poison day after day until our sensitivity to its damaging effects disappears? A foul word here, an untruth there and a sprinkling of criticism all combine in the slow poisoning process.

In the next five lessons, we will investigate some of the deadly effects that poisonous words can have, and we will learn about their antidotes to get the poison out of our systems.

Food
For Thought

"Do not remove a fly from your friend's
forehead with a hatchet."

(Chinese proverb)

"Criticism, like rain, should
be gentle enough to nourish a man's growth
without destroying his roots."

(Frank A. Clark)

"One of the hardest things to take is one of
the easiest things to give — criticism."

(Unknown)

"Any fool can criticize,
condemn and complain — and most do."

(Dale Carnegie)

"You can't let praise or criticism get to you.
It's a weakness to get caught up in either one."

(John Wooden)

Feed on God's Word

Look up these scriptures, and put in
your own words what they mean.

Proverbs 17:10

_____
_____
_____

Proverbs 27:5

_____
_____
_____

John 8:7

_____
_____
_____

1 Timothy 5:19-20

_____
_____
_____

Titus 3:2, 9

_____
_____
_____

Critical Words: Ready for a Roasting?

"He has a right to criticize who has the heart to help."
(Abraham Lincoln)

A class reunion can be a classic time for put-downs, intentional and otherwise. Often, more is roasted than the roast beef. On seeing a classmate we haven't seen in 10 or 20 years, our first impression seems to find its way to our lips before we know it. Seemingly innocuous comments tend to roll off the tongue: "You look so well preserved for your age"; "Looks like someone blew up your middle tire"; "Hasn't your hair turned a little redder over the last 20 years?"

Clearly, these grand slams will make impressions, but they won't be good. Although these critical words are veiled in humor, the insults are still there and eventually will find their mark. They are like the hidden barb of a fishhook. The first bite might be tasty, but soon the barb will snag its prey.

Tattletale, Tattletale!

Critical words find their way early to little tongues in the form of tattling. Adults need to know what goes on in a child's life, but some children believe they must give an up-to-the-minute report, especially concerning the misdeeds of other children. Young tattlers seem to need the assurance that a parent or teacher knows what is happening. It makes them feel good to tell about the misdeeds of someone else. Some people never outgrow this.

Adults tattle in different ways. They like to know what other people are doing and share with their friends tidbits of information. Any acquaintance with an open ear provides an audience for a rehearsal, usually with some embellishments, of the latest faults of another person.

Name-Calling

Although some adults would not maliciously criticize another person face to face, they find other ways to thrust in little jabs *absente reo* (the defendant being absent). Perhaps the most common example of this name-calling is when we're in the car. Someone pulls out in front of us. We might restrain from blasting him with our horn or even staring him down, but we frequently let the words flow: "What an idiot, creep, jerk, klutz … ." No wonder our children call other children names after hearing our colorful list of put-downs. Critical words hurt, whether they are heard firsthand or secondhand. They hurt the person who says them even if they are never heard by others.

Grumble and Gripe

Moses received his share of unwarranted criticism. He had just about had it with the complaining Israelites. After their miraculous trek across the Red Sea floor, they murmured about the bitter water at Marah (Exodus 15:22-24). That was the beginning of what seemed an endless stream of criticism against Moses' leadership. You name it, and they complained about it. They didn't like the food. They ran out of water. They thought Moses took too long on the mountain. They complained about their hardships. They were sick of manna. They questioned Moses' authority and grumbled that they would be slain by the giants of Canaan.

Note what Moses did when he was hit with this barrage of criticism. He reasoned with the unreasonable people the best he could. He prayed to God about the situation. He developed a thick skin. But most important, he didn't give up. Instead, he continued serving the Lord.

No one is immune to critical words. Even the perfect Son of God was criticized. Can we in our imperfection expect less? If we are alive, we probably will be criticized. Dogs usually bark at cars and other moving objects, not at gravestones. As Elbert Hubbard said, "To avoid criticism, do nothing, say nothing, be nothing."

Some people seem to think it is their duty to find fault in everyone and everything. Their incessant critical words can be compared to a form of medieval torture. The victim was restrained while a drop of water dripped on the same spot on his head. With each deliberate drop day after day, the victim was worn down and died a slow, agonizing death.

The constantly critical soul uses this vicious form of torture on its victims who must endure each stab and jab. This critical spirit can rear its malicious head in the workplace as supervisors bully employees and employees bully their supervisors. It can tear apart families as parents and children nit-pick each other to pieces. It can even appear in the church as members lambaste the preacher and leaders of the congregation. The critic is bent on destruction of spirit. Isn't there a better way?

Jesus' Way

In Matthew 18:15-17, Jesus showed us how to resolve a problem when someone has sinned against us. First, confront the individual in person. Second, if she doesn't listen, bring one or two other people to talk with him. Third, if she still will not listen, bring in the church to reason together.

Some people skip all these steps and immediately air their complaint for all to hear. Yet a real friend will speak the truth in love, making us aware of the problem and giving us an opportunity to correct it. "The kisses of an enemy may be profuse, but faithful are the wounds of a friend" (Proverbs 27:6).

Richard Walters called this negative feedback "beneficial bad news." He said, "We grow by changing the things we need to change, and we can't change them until we know about them." A friend's honest but kind advice can save us from future problems. "Perfume and incense bring joy to the heart, and the pleasantness of one's friend springs from his earnest counsel" (Proverbs 27:9).

In Galatians 6:1-5, Paul commented about the responsibility we have in criticizing: "Brothers, if someone is caught in a sin, you who are spiritual should restore him gently. But watch yourself, or you also may be tempted. Carry each other's burdens, and in this way you will fulfill the

Seasoning Your Words

law of Christ. If anyone thinks he is something when he is nothing, he deceives himself. Each one should test his own actions. Then he can take pride in himself, without comparing himself to somebody else, for each one should carry his own load."

Taking Criticism

So how do we respond to criticism in a Christlike manner? Here are some ways to help us deal with valid, and unwarranted, criticism:

Listen. We can't know whether criticism will help us until we hear what the other person is saying. The critic may be entirely wrong, but we can't judge until we have heard everything she has to say.

Consider. Think about what is said, and ask for clarification. James' advice is to be "quick to hear, slow to speak." Some truth might be spoken even if it is said in an inappropriate way. Try clarifying by restating: "So what you are saying is … ."

Don't retaliate. Sometimes we can reason with an accuser or complainer: "I'm sorry you feel that way." At other times silence might be the wiser response. When the recently crowned King Saul heard troublemakers doubting his ability, he held his anger (1 Samuel 11:12-13). At various times Jesus also met His accusers with silence and patience (Matthew 26:63; 27:12-14). Sometimes it is better not to try to reason with the unreasonable.

Develop a thick skin. Accepting yourself with your abilities and faults makes it easier to accept criticism from others. As Ruth Bell Graham observed, "Just pray for a tough hide and a tender heart."

Giving Criticism

Some people might find it more difficult to give criticism gracefully than to take it. The truth can hurt, even when it is spoken tactfully. How can we criticize more kindly?

Bite your tongue. Much criticism needs to go unsaid. Pause and consider whether your words will help or hurt. Is the problem one that really needs to be addressed, or does it need to be forgiven even before the person asks?

Get all the facts. Perhaps you don't know or understand the whole situation.

38

Pray don't find fault with the man who limps
Or stumbles along the road,
Unless you have worn the shoes he wears
Or struggled beneath his load.
There may be tacks in his shoes that hurt,
Though hidden away from view,
Or the burdens he bears, placed on your back,
Might cause you to stumble too.
– Unknown

Avoid "never" and other absolutes. Words such as "always," "everything," "totally" and "constantly" are overstatements. Rather, you might say, "Right now I believe …" or "At this particular time … ."

Be specific. In wartime, general bombing wipes out whole cities, but precision bombing destroys a strategic target as the rest of the city continues to function. Just so, specific criticism targets the problem; general criticism attacks the good as well as the bad.

Criticize one thing at a time. Companies have learned that employees find it difficult to conquer more than one problem at a time. Most people are frustrated and overwhelmed to be reprimanded for a multitude of faults; they can handle being challenged to work on one at a time more easily.

Include some praise with your criticism. Sincere praise softens the blow of criticism, but be sure the praise is deserved. One mother, looking hard for something to praise, congratulated her son for hitting only three people with the shopping cart. He had struck down six shoppers a week before.

The Minimizer
(or Shooting From the Lip)

Whether we are the critics or the criticized, may our words always be tempered with love.

You have heard of the Terminator, the Equalizer, the Eliminator? Well, now there's … the Minimizer!

The Minimizer

He rode into town that day,
Acting as if he were going to stay.
With silver spurs and 10-gallon hat,
Upon a proud horse he sat.

He swaggered down from his horse
And said, "Howdy," of course,
But then he got analytical,
And his words turned mighty critical.

"Why don't you ever paint your sign?
The lettering was sure out of line.
Can't you dress up the town a bit?
Looks pretty bad from where I sit!"

This cowboy liked to cut things down;
He minimized folks all over town.
It wasn't with his gun he killed;
His mouth – that's where he was skilled.

He criticized the barber's cut.
In the road he saw every rut.
Aunt Mertie's dumplings he denounced.
The mayor's politics he trounced.

The saloon doors were much too squeaky,
And the floor was way too creaky.
The bank's rates were much too high.
He made plain Jane Stenson cry.

The townspeople endured this critical stuff.
They suffered till they'd had enough.
They formed a posse late one night
And rode the "Minimizer" out of sight.

It's not how tall in the saddle he sat,
How his spurs jingled, how he cocked his hat,
Nor how famous he was from North to South;
No, it mattered how he managed his mouth!

Think About It

1. Explain how Moses handled criticism.

2. What was Jesus' method of giving criticism?

3. What happened to the grumblers who spread a bad report about Canaan (Numbers 14:36-37)?

4. How did David deal with the cursings from Shimei, and why (2 Samuel 16:5-14)?

5. "As iron sharpens iron, so one man sharpens another" (Proverbs 27:17). How can we sharpen each other without being harmful?

6. How can a rebuker be more appreciated than a flatterer (Proverbs 28:23)?

7. How did Nehemiah deal with Sanballat and Tobiah when they tried to ridicule his work in rebuilding the walls of Jerusalem (Nehemiah 2:19-20; 4; 6:1-14)?

8. How did Priscilla and Aquila deal with Apollos and his erroneous teaching (Acts 18:24-26)?

9. What blessing does one have who rescues a wanderer from the truth (James 5:19-20)?

10. How did Jude describe the "grumblers and faultfinders" (Jude 16)?

Food
For Thought

"What is intended as a little white lie often
ends up as a double feature in technicolor."

(Madena R. Wallingford)

"The telling of a falsehood is like
the cut of a saber; for though the wound may heal,
the scar of it will remain."

(Saadi)

"Truth, like oil in water,
will eventually come to the surface."

(Unknown)

"In a time of universal deceit —
telling the truth is a revolutionary act."

(George Orwell)

"Men occasionally stumble over the truth,
but most of them pick themselves up and hurry
off as if nothing ever happened."

(Winston Churchill)

Feed on God's Word

Look up these scriptures, and put in
your own words what they mean.

Proverbs 14:5

_____
_____
_____

Proverbs 12:19, 22

_____
_____
_____

Proverbs 24:26

_____
_____
_____

Proverbs 25:18

_____
_____
_____

Proverbs 26:18-19, 28

_____
_____
_____

Untrue Words:
Another Fish Story

"If you tell the truth,
you don't have to remember anything."
(Mark Twain)

"**A**nd the fish I caught was this big ... or was it this big?" the fisherman questions himself, as he stretches the imaginary length two more inches. Some fishermen have a knack for telling stories. Some of their tales are of medium height, but many of them are quite tall.

We chuckle at fish stories, but in reality, telling untruths is no laughing matter. God makes clear in His Word that liars will not enter heaven (Revelation 21:8). To God, a lie is a lie – period. He does not qualify lies by little, big, black or white. In John 8:44-47, Jesus implied that people who lie are the devil's children. He called the devil "the father of lies" and says that lying is "his native language." Some of us might not be wild about our relatives, but the devil is someone we surely don't want in our family.

John said, "The man who says, 'I know him,' but does not do what he commands is a liar, and the truth is not in him" (1 John 2:4). Our credibility is based not only on what we say but also on what we do. Throughout His ministry Jesus stressed that His followers must practice what they preach. Often He chastised the Pharisees for their deceitful words and hearts. They lived a lie. They said one thing but showed by their actions that their hearts were not right. Appropriately, Jesus

45

repeated Isaiah's indictment of the Jews centuries before: "These people honor me with their lips, but their hearts are far from me" (Matthew 15:8; cf. Isaiah 29:13). In Matthew 23 Jesus rebuked the scribes and Pharisees for their say-one-thing-do-another lives. It is much like the hypocrisy about which David spoke: "They take delight in lies. With their mouths they bless, but in their hearts they curse" (Psalm 62:4).

Deceit Destroys

Lies have precipitated the downfall of good people. A case in point is found in 1 Kings 13. Israel's King Jeroboam was busy building golden calves in Dan and Bethel. He didn't want the people of Israel going to Jerusalem to worship, thus giving their allegiance back to King Rehoboam. God sent a "man of God" to condemn Jeroboam, who was standing by the altar to burn incense.

The man of God declined Jeroboam's dinner invitation because of the Lord's command that he was not to "eat bread or drink water or return by the way" he had come (1 Kings 13:9). In that culture, partaking of food together could signify establishment of a covenant. Perhaps God wanted to symbolize His displeasure with Jeroboam's sin by having the man of God refuse to eat a meal.

An old prophet living in Bethel invited the man of God to his home. When the man of God refused, the old prophet lied, saying that an angel had told him to invite the man of God. The man of God ate and drank with the old man but later was killed by a lion.

Why did the old prophet lie? To enhance his prestige? To entertain a visitor to Jeroboam? To enjoy the companionship of another prophet? To see if he could cause the man of God to stumble? The Scriptures are not clear regarding his motive. We only know the result of his lie. The man of God should have been true to his purpose. How easy it was for him to believe a lie. How easy it is for us to do the same today.

Getting the Story Crooked

For many people, telling the truth doesn't seem to be as important as it used to be. One 2002 study at the University of Massachusetts found that 60 percent of adults could not have a 10-minute conversation without lying. In fact, those that lied averaged as least three lies during their chat. Later when their conversations were replayed, they were shocked at how often they lied. People might not set out to be liars but sometimes they just don't tell the whole truth or they fudge just a little. Take, for example, a 2007 *Scientific American* study that found 90 percent of people lied when they filled out their online dating profile to get matched with a date. The most obvious lie for women was posting their weight at 8½ pounds lighter than they really were. On the other hand, men lied to look richer, taller and/or better educated in order to attract the perfect date.

Why do people lie anyway? When children are young, they fantasize and tell stories about imaginary friends or places. Usually, these instances are isolated and are just a facet of a child's active imagination.

As a child begins to learn about right and wrong, he also learns about consequences. He fears that if he tells the truth about his misbehavior, something bad will happen to him, that he will not be loved. Fibbing is often a spontaneous attempt to cover up little imperfections.

Some parents make it easy – almost advantageous – for their children to lie. When suspected for some misdeed, the kids are questioned, "Who did this?" Little eyes shift while voices quiver, "Not me!" Maybe "What happened?" would be a wiser question for parents to ask to find out about misbehavior without encouraging a lie.

Often when children tell the truth about a transgression, their parents pounce on the error without appreciating the fact that the truth was told. Children must know that telling the truth is expected. Telling the truth does not always mean they will escape the consequences of their actions. A lie may fool mom or dad, but God always knows the truth. Above all, parents must always make sure that their children know they are loved by their family and by God.

Some people never grow out of the fibbing stage and go on to become chronic liars. They fear that people will not like them for who they really are. Always being afraid of being found out, they live in a shell of delusions.

We don't always have to tell all we know or feel. We can be direct without revealing our innermost thoughts. If someone asks another person how she is, she can answer, "Fine," referring to her general health without going into a 15-minute recital of his painful ingrown toenail, marital problems and financial crisis.

What if telling the truth means hurting someone's feelings? An old

Arab proverb says, "When you shoot an arrow of truth, dip its point in honey." Our discretion comes into play here. Many times we have the choice of being silent or speaking the truth in love. As Henry David Thoreau said, "The only way to speak the truth is to speak lovingly."

The Trouble With Cross-Stitch

I enjoy cross-stitching, especially counted cross-stitch. But I have learned that this creative process is also an exacting one. Once as I was working on a complicated design, I miscalculated the number of stitches. "No problem," I thought, "I'll just make up the difference on the other side of the pattern." Unfortunately, when I made the minor change on that side, it altered the top and bottom. The total design was affected although the alterations were relatively small.

Lying is like that. You cannot make a little alteration in a fact without its affecting another fact and then another. Finally, the whole design of life is altered by that first fabrication. Each untruth builds on the next. Even a little lie can make a big difference. Paul admonished, "Therefore each of you must put off falsehood and speak truthfully to his neighbor, for we are all members of one body" (Ephesians 4:25).

What's Your Credibility Quotient?

How credible are you, really? Do you say what you mean? Do you do what you say? Take this test and see.

1. Do you tell a companion to say you are not at home when you do not want to speak to a caller on the phone?

2. Do you fudge a little about your qualifications in a job interview?

3. Do you assure someone you will pray for her and her needs but then forget all about it?

4. When your friend or spouse reminds you about the speed limit and asks you how fast you are going, do you tell him a lower speed just to get him off your back?

5. Do you say you will play with the children but later tell them you are not in the mood?

6. Do you tell one friend one thing and another friend something else just to make them happy?

7. Do you fib about the age of a small-sized child to get a cheaper entrance price at a park or movie?

8. Do you intentionally downgrade yourself or your family's abilities so that another will praise you?

9. Do you quote someone erroneously and out of context to support your particular viewpoint?

10. Do you intentionally exaggerate the size of crowds in worship, the speed of your car or the weight of your baby?

In their book *Family Feelings*, Martha Vanceburg and Sylvia W. Silverman wrote about the importance of truth in our daily lives:

> "We can't save ethics for a rainy day. That's like saying we can lie all week and tell the truth on Sunday. Ethics are like shoes: if we save our good ones for special occasions, we won't ever be comfortable with them. But if we wear poor shoes all the time, our feet will give us trouble. Honesty and integrity should be worn every day, and if honesty compels us to heed a different drummer, then that's the rhythm we march to" (p. 27).

Think About It

1. "An excuse is a thin skin of falsehood stretched tightly over a bold-faced lie" (Unknown). Do you agree? Explain.

2. Who is the father of lies (John 8:44)? Who is Truth (John 14: 6)?

3. Why do you think the old prophet of Bethel lied? Did he ever admit his error (1 Kings 13)?

4. What are some ways to encourage children to tell the truth?

5. Are being direct and being honest the same thing?

6. What's the difference between flattery and a compliment?

7. Find instances in the Bible where the phrase "false witness" is used.

8. What was the sin involved when Ananias and Sapphira gave their gift to the apostles (Acts 5:1-11)?

9. Who told the first lie in the Bible (Genesis 3:1-4)?

10. Is lying ever justified?

Food
For Thought

"*Anger is often more hurtful than
the injury that caused it.*"

(Yiddish proverb)

"*Forgiveness saves the expense of anger,
the cost of hatred, and the waste of energy.*"

(Unknown)

"*Anger is one letter short of danger.*"

(Unknown)

"*Before you give someone a piece of your mind,
make sure you have enough to spare.*"

(Unknown)

"*For every minute you remain angry,
you give up 60 seconds of peace of mind.*"

(Ralph Waldo Emerson)

Feed on God's Word

Look up these scriptures, and put in
your own words what they mean.

Proverbs 15:1

_____
_____
_____

Proverbs 16:32

_____
_____
_____

Proverbs 29:11, 22

_____
_____
_____

Ecclesiastes 7:9

_____
_____
_____

1 Peter 3:9-10

_____
_____
_____

Angry Words:
Letting the Steam Out of the Pressure Cooker

"Everyone should be quick to listen, slow to speak and slow to become angry, for man's anger does not bring about the righteous life that God desires" (James 1:19-20).

Modern technology has given us thousands of kitchen conveniences; one of these is the pressure cooker. Intensive inner pressure causes foods to cook in a fraction of the time required by a conventional pot. That pressure must be maintained, however, for the process to work properly. If the lid is capped on carelessly, the steam continually escapes and cooking occurs much more slowly. If the lid is fastened tightly with no release of pressure, the pot will explode. But if correct amounts of steam and pressure are regulated, food can be cooked efficiently and well.

So it is with the pressure cooker of our emotions. The emotion of anger will manifest itself in some way. If we constantly vent our anger on other people, productive relationships will be difficult. On the other hand, if anger is contained so that there is no release it will eventually explode. If regulated outlets can be found for our anger, then we can vent our anger effectively in a healthy manner.

Our physical response to anger is involuntary and occurs whether we wish it or not. When the body feels endangered, disturbed or angry, the fight-or-flight mechanism prepares it for action. This defense system of the body causes adrenaline to pour into the bloodstream. Blood pressure increases with the acceleration of the heartbeat. The muscles have a sudden burst of energy. In seconds, a person can go from quiet to an alarm reaction state. These intense feelings are impossible to ignore. Fortunately, our reaction to these feelings of anger can be controlled.

Is Anger Sin?

"In your anger do not sin" (Ephesians 4:26). Is it sinful to be angry? How can a person be angry and not sin?

Studying God's Word gives us a better understanding of anger. Richard Walters said the Bible mentions God's anger about four times more often than man's anger. In many instances God and Jesus expressed anger, yet They are perfect.

Anger is a God-given emotion, like joy or sorrow. Anger is not good or bad in and of itself. It is simply an emotion that is triggered when we think something is wrong. How we react to anger can be right or wrong. Anger should lead us to action that is motivated by love, but often anger leads us to hateful actions that only destroy. Our reaction to anger depends greatly on our relationship with God and the growth of the fruit of the Spirit in our hearts. Let's look at three biblical examples of dealing with anger.

Three Biblical Examples

John, the apostle of love, was not always such an admirable example. Jesus nicknamed him and his brother James "Sons of Thunder," or as Walters said, "a more literal translation suggests, 'the Soon-angry Ones' (Mark 3:17)." When a Samaritan village refused hospitality to Jesus and His tired disciples, James and John became enraged. Remembering how the fiery Elijah called down fire on the soldiers (2 Kings 1:9-12), they promptly demanded that Jesus use the same terminator approach on the Samaritans. Jesus rebuked their outburst (Luke 9:54-55).

In 2 Samuel 13 we read about the simmering resentment of Absalom. His sister Tamar had been seduced and raped by their half-brother Amnon. Although their father David was furious with Amnon's actions, we never read about his taking any disciplinary action against Amnon. Absalom decided to take revenge into his own hands. He said not a word to Amnon but smoldered in hatred for two years. Finally, he made an opportunity to strike back. At Absalom's feast, Amnon was struck down by Absalom's men (vv. 28-29).

In contrast to John and Absalom, consider the indignation of Amos. Self-described as a shepherd and caretaker of sycamore-fig trees, Amos was called by the Lord to prophesy to the Northern Kingdom (Amos 7:14-15). His mission brought him from the wilderness near his home of Tekoa to the streets of Bethel. There in the shadow of the royal palace of Jeroboam II, the excesses of the nation became quickly apparent. Wealth and greed quenched any spiritual fervor. Might became right. Corruption in government and business was rampant. While the poor suffered, the rich were "complacent in Zion" (Amos 6:1). God and true worship were forgotten.

Amos, although untutored as a prophet, spoke out as God's instrument against religious apathy. Amos' anger at the injustices of Israel caused him to act, to speak up, to do something about the wrongs he witnessed.

These three examples demonstrate rage, resentment and indignation. John's words lashed out in rage to harm. Absalom spoke not a word but seethed in his anger and resentment. Amos' indignation was directed at the sin, not the sinner. These reactions are summarized below:

Rage	*Resentment*	*Indignation*
Seeks to do wrong	*Seeks to hide wrong*	*Seeks to correct wrong*
Guided by selfishness	*Guided by cowardice*	*Guided by mercy*
Seeks vengeance	*Seeks vengeance*	*Seeks justice*
Wages open warfare	*Wages guerrilla war*	*Defends truth*
Defends itself	*Defends the status quo*	*Defends the other person*
Forbidden by Bible	*Forbidden by Bible*	*Required by Bible*
Destroys people	*Destroys people*	*Destroys evil*

(Adapted from Walters, Richard. Anger, Yours and Mine, and What to Do About It, *p. 17)*

Just as steam escapes in various ways from a pressure cooker, so the expression of anger takes many forms in different people – psychosomatic illness, violence, suicide, depression, overwork, overeating or even saccharin kindness. Some people seem to have a short fuse, but others seem to let nothing bother them. God asks self-control from all Christians, whatever their emotional make-up or background.

Immediate First Aid

How do we control our anger without its controlling us? Here are some immediate first-aid procedures – temporary measures for on-the-spot relief of destructive angry responses.

Admit you are angry. Anger is a natural emotion. Don't deny or suppress it if it's there.

Ask God's help in prayer. Pray for a forgiving heart, one full of patience and peace. Pray for the other person who is angry with you or with whom you are angry.

Read and meditate on Scripture. Fill your mind with good things rather than thoughts of revenge or hate.

Measure the issue. Is it worth being angry about? Perhaps after reflection, you will determine that the offense is not as serious as it seems. Maybe the matter could be resolved in your heart without further concern.

Control yourself. Have you ever had to answer the phone in the middle of an angry exchange? Your tone changes, and you swiftly shift gears. This proves we often can control our angry words if we try.

Relax. Take a deep breath. Close your eyes. Count to 10. Give yourself a chance to regain composure.

Find harmless outlets. Punching a bag or pounding a pillow can be therapeutic, but it would be better still if the energy used in these activities could be channeled into something constructive. Some people calm down by playing a quiet game or by listening to soothing music. Other people work out their anger by exercising or starting a new project they always have wanted to try. But visualizing the death or destruction of the person with whom one is angry or acting out such a death by throwing darts at his picture or sticking pins in a doll is unhealthy.

First-aid measures to overcome anger are temporary at best. We won't avoid anger entirely, but we need to resolve the causes of our anger and prevent them if possible.

Ongoing Treatment

Treating a lifetime of suppressed or repressed anger requires more than simple first-aid. Some wounds have been festering so long that professional help might be required to help one start the healing process. Ongoing care is necessary to sustain a healthier soul.

Don't stay angry too long. "Do not let the sun go down while you are still angry, and do not give the devil a foothold" (Ephesians 4:26-27). Find some ways to resolve the anger in your heart. Anger festers if it is not resolved.

Talk to the other person involved as soon as possible. Apologize and make restitution if necessary. No matter who is at fault, each Christian has the responsibility to start the reconciliation process (Matthew 5:23-26; Mark 11:25). Think how the world would be if everyone were willing to talk and clear up her differences with other people.

Talk to an understanding friend. Sometimes it isn't wise or possible to encounter the person with whom we have had conflict. By voicing our concerns to an objective observer, we might be able to see clearer solutions to problems. We must be careful to talk to trustworthy people who will not spread tales about our conflicts to other people.

Stay physically healthy. By taking care of our bodies with adequate exercise, diet and rest, we will be more resilient to stress and thus can ward off the anger it can bring.

Learn how pressure builds in ourselves and other people. By understanding our pressure points and relief valves, we can possibly avoid or decrease the frequency of uncomfortable situations. Why flirt with trouble unnecessarily?

Forgive. God sometimes permits frustrating things to happen to us to teach us patience and maturity. As Paul reminded the Colossians, "Bear with each other and forgive whatever grievances you may have against one another. Forgive as the Lord forgave you" (Colossians 3:13). No offense committed by another person could in any way equal our guilt before God, yet He has forgiven us freely (Ephesians 4:31-32). Should we not then be willing to show that same mercy to other people? As Walters concluded,

> "By studying anger and its power, we can learn self-control so that we do not need to lose our temper in rage or abuse ourselves with resentment, but can defuse anger by resolving circumstances and then use the energy of anger through Christlike indignation" (p. 149).

Think About It

1. Which kind of anger (rage, resentment or indignation) played a part in these biblical events:

   a. The first murder (Genesis 4:5)

   b. Death of Shechemites (Genesis 34:25-26; 49:5-7)

   c. Moses' seeing the golden calf (Exodus 32:19-20)

   d. Samson's killing 30 men at Ashkelon (Judges 14:19)

   e. Saul's reaction to the news from Jabesh Gilead (1 Samuel 11:6)

   f. Eliab's rebuke to David (1 Samuel 17:28)

   g. Saul and Jonathan's disagreement (1 Samuel 20:30-34)

   h. Xerxes' reaction when Queen Vashti didn't come (Esther 1:12)

   i. Jonah's distress when God did not destroy Nineveh (Jonah 4:1-4)

   j. Nehemiah's reaction to the outcries of the poor (Nehemiah 5:6)

2. List the causes of God's anger in these scriptures.

   a. Exodus 4:14

   b. Numbers 11:1, 10; 12:9

   c. Numbers 25:3-4

   d. Numbers 31:1-3

   e. Deuteronomy 7:3-4

   f. Judges 2:12-14, 20; 3:7-8; 10:6-7

   g. 2 Samuel 6:7-11

   h. 2 Samuel 24

   i. 2 Chronicles 25:15

   j. Isaiah 30:27-33

3. List the causes of Christ's anger in these scriptures.

   a. Mark 3:5

   b. Mark 11:15-17

   c. Mark 13:14

Food
For Thought

"*If you wouldn't write it and sign it, don't say it.*"
(Unknown)

"*Bathroom humor should be flushed down the toilet.*"
(Unknown)

"*A holy mind cannot repeat a vile thing,
let alone be the creator of a vile suggestion.*"
(John G. Lake)

"*The foolish and wicked practice of profane cursing
and swearing is a vice so mean and low that every
person of sense and character detests and despises it.*"
(George Washington)

"*Writers used to make such wonderful pictures
without all that swearing, all that cursing.
And now it seems that you can't say
three words without cursing.*"
(Ernest Borgnine)

Feed on God's Word

Look up these scriptures, and put in
your own words what they mean.

Exodus 21:17

_____

_____

_____

Deuteronomy 5:11

_____

_____

_____

Psalm 111:9

_____

_____

_____

Proverbs 16:27

_____

_____

_____

Matthew 15:10-11

_____

_____

_____

#6

Offensive Words: Cooking the Frog

"Nor should there be obscenity, foolish talk or coarse joking, which are out of place, but rather thanksgiving"
(Ephesians 5:4).

*I*f you put a frog in cold water and gradually increase the temperature, he will stay there until he dies. He could jump out at any time, but with a slow rise in temperature, the frog doesn't notice the change. He just sits there and gets cooked.

Our frog has been cooked in the realm of offensive language – words that are profane and obscene. Gradually, we have become accustomed to hearing words that deride and shame God and people. These words don't bother us as they once did. Hearing or even saying them doesn't seem quite so bad.

Today society holds little regard for the third of the Ten Commandments, which forbids taking God's name in vain (Exodus 20:7). Unlike Moses, who showed reverence for the "I AM" by removing his shoes, people today are more likely to trample God's name underfoot. Respect for God and His name have fallen by the wayside.

At one time the Jews refused to speak God's name when they read from the scrolls because they feared they might say it irreverently. Such respect is a far cry from the frivolous manner in which the name of God is invoked indiscriminately in the most mundane affairs today.

The Swearing Disciple

Peter was probably known among the disciples for his impulsive spirit and quick tongue. When Christ predicted that all His followers would scatter the night of His betrayal, Peter countered that he would be the exception. Christ told Peter that he would disown his Lord three times before the cock crowed. Peter flatly denied such a prophecy, as did the other disciples (Matthew 26:31-35).

Later as Peter warmed himself by the fire in the courtyard outside the judgment hall where Jesus was on trial, several people began to question this obvious foreigner. Ironically, it was Peter's Galilean accent that gave them a clue to his origin and possible connection with the accused prisoner on trial (Matthew 26:73).

But under the pressure of the situation, Peter did all he could to deny any friendship with Jesus. Because his talk gave him away, he would prove by his speech that he wasn't a disciple of the Lord. After a simple denial didn't seem to quell the accusations, Peter added an oath and finally cursing and swearing. "Then he began to call down curses on himself and he swore to them, 'I don't know the man!'" (Matthew 26:74). He was swearing almost before he was aware of it. His example shows how rapidly offensive words can escape the tongue. A piercing look from the Lord brought Peter to his senses and to tears (Luke 22:61-62).

"But It's Just a Byword"

People still reproach Christ by their language, sometimes intentionally and sometimes not. Many of our so-called innocent bywords, which may be uttered in ignorance, can be traced to curse words. They have become accepted because they are not technically swear words. Spouting these off releases pressure and tension without seeming to be bad. If these bywords are analyzed, however, one can see their roots.

This list shows swear words and some of their probable derived bywords.

Hell	Heck
God	Golly, gosh, ye gad, gad, goodness, gracious, good grief, great guns
Lord, have mercy	Lord, lordy mercy, lausy mercy, my law
Damn	Dang, darn, dern

Jehovah	Great Jehosophat
Jesus Christ	Judas Priest, Criminy Christmas, Jeeez

In Matthew 5:34-37 Jesus said, "But I tell you, Do not swear at all: either by heaven, for it is God's throne; or by the earth, for it is his footstool; or by Jerusalem, for it is the city of the Great King. And do not swear by your head, for you cannot make even one hair white or black. Simply let your 'Yes' be 'Yes,' and your 'No,' 'No'; anything beyond this comes from the evil one."

Look at the bywords that have been devised for swearing:

I swear	I swany
by heaven	my heavens, heavens above, heavenly days, heaven help us, heaven forbid
by the judgment	great day, great day in the morning
by Earth	my lands, land of Goshen, my landy mercy, lands' sake, what in the world
by Jerusalem	gee, gee-whiz, geerusalem

Some terms have been transposed and abbreviated to make them more palatable. "Dog" is substituted for "God," and some resulting phrases are: dog-goned, dog-take-it, dag-nab-it, dad-burn-it, dad-blast-it, gold-dern-it. Through texting, abbreviations such as OMG have been created to mean "Oh My God."

"But I Don't Mean It!"

"But I don't mean anything bad when I say those words!" some people will say. That's the point. The casual, thoughtless use of God's name or a similar replacement still demonstrates a lack of reverence for Him, as if the user is not taking God seriously. What is the purpose of saying these bywords, after all? Aren't they uttered at times of surprise, anger or hurt – the same times swear words would be used? The similarity of these expressions is difficult to deny. Although the intent might not be the same, the watered-down swearing is still there. This truth is quite incriminating, especially if we have used these expressions innocently.

"But everybody uses those expressions," someone counters. Does that make it right? Are we letting other people set our standard of speech? A factory manager daily paused in front of a watchmaker's shop to check the time on the clocks in the window. He was responsible for blowing the whistle for lunchtime. Little did he know that the watchmaker had been setting his clocks by the noon whistle each day. Unknowingly, they had been using each other's time as their standard.

We come to understand better what James meant when he said that the man who controls his tongue is a perfect man (James 3:2). For many people, conquest of the tongue is the most difficult challenge, the last frontier of evil worlds to conquer. We must be on guard constantly to bridle our tongues, and we can be thankful that God has given us the assurance that He will help us. He asks us to be as pure as we can be: "Avoid every kind of evil" (1 Thessalonians 5:22). The tongue is a good place to start.

Has Clean Speech Gone With the Wind?

Public profanity has moved from disgrace to center stage with help from the entertainment industry. It seems as if clean language has been "gone with the wind" ever since censors approved Rhett Butler's profane parting farewell to Scarlett O'Hara in 1939. Profanity is no longer shocking in movies, but added to avoid "G" ratings. Humor is often dependent on blaspheming God's name.

Even television is full of language that makes Clark Gable's single profanity seem tame. Cursing is commonplace in prime-time shows. Talk shows that used to "bleep" profanities include them in the host's monologue. Even the network news is not immune.

Rather than teaching values like teamwork and practice, some athletes on television model rage and vulgarity. Close up shots of enraged athletes and coaches cursing at the officials are commonplace. Athletes who once thanked God in post-game interviews now curse at owners and fans. One coach tried to make his problem into a joke "I took up tennis, which made me bilingual – English and profanity. The last three years, I've taken up golf and English has become a second language."

Profanity and vulgarity became so bad in the music industry that warning labels are now attached to many recordings. Songs that glorify suicide, incest, rape, sadomasochism and the occult are often heard. Too many teens have followed in the footsteps of their musical heroes, living fast and dying young.

Much of rap music has reached new depths in vulgarity. The lyrics exalt vile language, rampant drug use and the degradation of women. It is not just rap music that is vulgar. Just listen to the words of some popular "cheatin' and drinkin' " country songs or the "partyin'" pop songs.

Rooting Through the Garbage

Many people might say, "It [the book, movie, TV show] was good except for some dirty language." What do we have to dig through to get to the good part? A garbage dump might have some good food in it, but who wants to wade through the filth to find it? If our minds have to swim in the sewer to retrieve the quality in something, then we can't escape the stench of the foul as well. Our minds have no garbage disposal, in which a flick of the switch flushes away unwanted trash. Rather, our minds store impressions, sometimes for a lifetime. We should expose them only to the best. "If enough of us say no to conversational garbage, the whole world will smell better," Richard Walters explained.

Public outcry against some of the rampant sex, violence and profanity in the media has had some effect. Like movies, TV programs and video games carry ratings, and the most vulgar recordings have parental warning labels. Add to this mix more than a billion websites on the Internet. No wonder it's a real challenge to sort through and screen out obscene videos and movies. To combat these influences, parents need to model the proper online behavior themselves and teach their children what is acceptable. As much as possible, parents need to be aware of what is being seen and heard. Some families install parental control software that filters, blocks and even monitors inappropriate websites for their children's protection.

Great harm or good can be done by words spoken through the media. There are wholesome shows and music that provide family entertainment and help in teaching values. The media is like fire; used correctly it keeps us warm, cooks our food and helps us see at night. But used foolishly, it wrecks havoc. As James said: "Consider what a great forest is set on fire by a small spark. The tongue also is a fire, a world of evil among the parts of the body. It corrupts the whole person, sets the whole course of his life on fire, and is itself set on fire by hell" (James 3:5-6).

Cleaning Up

You can turn off the television, skip the movie, or refuse to buy the CD or download the music. But what do you do about a foul-mouthed co-worker or neighbor with whom you must associate day after day? It becomes difficult to tune out every comment, especially if you have no choice regarding the association. Selective listening is an art to be cultivated, but the onslaught of garbage dumping in our ears has to take its toll.

How does one clean up her speech and keep it that way?

Admit vulnerability. In certain circumstances we will be tempted to utter foul language. We need to be on guard especially during those vulnerable times.

Limit exposure. Some situations are unavoidable, but when we are given a choice, we can cut down on opportunities to hear dirty speech. We can decline to listen to trash talk and move on to another subject or leave the area where such talk is spoken. While rejecting the action, we can accept the speaker. One might say, "The joke about those people doesn't particularly interest me. Say, how is your redecorating coming?"

Find alternatives to bywords and swear words. With creativity we can find words that express how we feel without being offensive to God. For example, you could say how you really feel like "I can't believe it!" or "That hurt!" How about something harmless or nonsensical that you make up? Or you could say nothing but expend some energy by stretching your foot or leaving the area if you can. Take some time to think ahead so you won't be caught off guard like the apostle Peter.

Show respect. We need to strive to show more reverence regarding God and His Word, whether in words or actions. Paul wrote, "Let us purify ourselves from everything that contaminates body and spirit, perfecting holiness out of reverence for God" (2 Corinthians 7:1).

Elihu Root, secretary of state in the early 1900s, once said, "Words are like those insects that take their color from their surroundings." What hue do your surroundings cast on your words? How shady are your frequent companions and their words? Are the words off-color in the books you read, the movies you see and the TV shows you watch? What color are your words?

Think About It

1. What are some reasons children might use foul language?

2. Give examples of Peter's impulsive nature (Matthew 14:25-33; 26:31-35; John 18:10-11).

3. What punishment was required of the son who blasphemed God's name (Leviticus 24:10-23)?

4. How did David describe the Lord's name in Psalm 8:1?

5. On several occasions the Jewish leaders accused Jesus of blasphemy (Matthew 9:3-8; 26:63-66; John 10:31-39). Why was He innocent?

6. What did Jesus tell us to do to people who curse us (Luke 6:28)?

7. What did Paul tell us to do to people who persecute us (Romans 12:14)?

8. What positive advice did James give to prevent us from swearing (James 5:12)?

9. When persecuting the early Christians, what had Paul tried to force them to do (Acts 26:11)? What did he later call himself (1 Timothy 1:13)?

10. What are some ways to screen the movies and TV programs that we and our children watch?

Food For Thought

"The trouble with people who talk too fast
is that they often say something
they haven't thought about yet."

(Unknown)

"I will never repeat gossip,
so please listen carefully the first time."

(Unknown)

"Great minds talk about ideas.
Average minds talk about things.
Small minds talk about people."

(Unknown)

"Prejudice is a learned trait.
You're not born prejudiced; you're taught it."

(Charles R. Swindoll)

"I just wish my mouth had a backspace key."

(Unknown)

69

Feed on God's Word

Look up these scriptures, and put in
your own words what they mean.

Proverbs 17:9

_____
_____
_____

Proverbs 20:19, 25

_____
_____
_____

Proverbs 26:17, 20

_____
_____
_____

Ecclesiastes 5:2-3

_____
_____
_____

Ecclesiastes 10:20

_____
_____
_____

Careless Words:
Slippery Tongue Anyone?

"Conversation between Adam and Eve must have been difficult at times because they had nobody to talk about."
(Agnes Repplier)

I am a monster. I maim and destroy, yet gain strength with age. I am malicious and cunning. My helpless victims cannot protect themselves from me because I have no face. I am nearly impossible to track. I become more elusive the more I am sought. I cause indigestion, heartache and sleepless nights. I tear families apart and topple governments. My name? Careless Words.

Careless words – the words that role off slippery tongues without much thought, concern or wisdom – can do more damage than we think. During World War II the government feared that a word lightly spoken to a "friend" might result in a sunken ship or a surprise attack. Posters of the day sent warnings: "Be like Dad – keep Mum! Careless talk costs lives." "Many lives were lost in the last war through careless talk. Be on your guard! Don't discuss movements of ships or troops." "Loose lips sink ships."

Wartime isn't the only time to watch our careless words. Some people seem to have a perpetual case of hoof-and-mouth disease; they are continually hoofing over to their neighbor and mouthing. They start their mouths before their brains are put in gear.

In *The Quest for Character*, Charles Swindoll expresses well the danger of this tendency to utter careless words:

> How much hurt, how much damage can be done by chance remarks! Our unguarded tongues can deposit germ-thoughts of hurt, humiliation, and hate into tender minds which fester, become full-blown infections, and ultimately spread disease throughout an adult personality. With little regard for the other person's vulnerability, we have the power to initiate a violent emotional earthquake by merely making a few statements that rip and tear like shrapnel in the person's head. Such destructive words are like sending 800 volts through 110 wire (p. 45).

You Can't Take Them Back

Careless words have a unique way of being irreversible. Just saying, "I take them back," will not reverse their meaning. Once words are spoken, no matter how badly we wish we hadn't said them, we cannot take them back. Like a bee sting, you can remove the stinger, but the poison remains.

When a judge directs a jury to "disregard the last statement made by the witness," the instruction does not mean the words can be obliterated from the minds of the jurors. The seeds of suspicion have been planted, and any sly lawyer knows they are difficult to remove.

Jesus considered careless words a serious matter. He charged, "But I tell you that men will have to give account on the day of judgment for every careless word they have spoken. For by your words you will be acquitted, and by your words you will be condemned" (Matthew 12:36-37). The fact that our words could determine our eternal destiny makes them of great importance indeed.

Consider this example of a person who lost someone precious because of his careless words.

A Foolish Promise

Reckless and courageous, Jephthah was a man of the hour. After being cast out of his homeland (Judges 11:1-2), he found himself being begged to return as commander of the Israelite army against the Ammonites. To make certain that he would not be ousted again, Jephthah made the elders promise to keep him as their leader and to make the commitment binding.

Jephthah decided to make a promise of his own. He vowed to offer whatever first came out of his house to meet him if the Lord made him victorious in battle (Judges 11:30-31). Although he lived in the pagan land of Tob, he knew he needed God's help to win over his enemies.

What Jephthah didn't know was that his only daughter would be the first one out the door to meet him after his victory. His heart was broken because of his foolish words, but he had to follow through on his promise (Leviticus 5:4). His daughter agreed to be sacrificed. After she spent a period in mourning, "he did to her as he had vowed" (Judges 11:39).

Many questions surround this sad story about Jephthah. Did Jephthah originally intend to sacrifice a human on the altar, or was he thinking only about an animal sacrifice? Did he fulfill his promise to God by slaying his only daughter, or did he commit her to perpetual virginity in service to the tabernacle? Why was such a man of undesirable parentage and reputation chosen to lead God's people in the first place?

One thing is certain: Jephthah made a rash vow. His careless words, spoken in the heat of patriotic zeal, resulted in heartache for his daughter and himself. This blow hit harder than any he had received in battle.

We can learn from Jephthah that it is wise to make our promises few and to commit ourselves to carrying out the ones we do make. Perhaps a better policy would be not to make promises at all. Then they cannot be broken (Deuteronomy 23:21-23).

Jephthah's foolish words backfired with tragic results. Other types of careless words can also wreak havoc and despair.

Words That Backfire

When airplanes were first used in World War I, pilots attempted to shoot down their enemies with hand-held guns. Meeting with little success, they began to use machine guns. They tried to fire these forward, but the propellers were in the way. A French flyer wrapped the propeller blades in steel-wire tape to prevent the blades from being riddled by the bullets. To his horror, the bullets ricocheted off the blades and killed two of his companions in the cockpit.

Gossip backfires just as those bullets did. How many times have whispered, derogatory words come back to haunt us? Gossip is supposedly protected because of concern for the people involved, but this concern is just a cloud cover for sin. "I heard," "They say," "I wonder," and "Did you know?" may be beginnings to slurs on character or questions of motives.

John gives us one possible motive for gossiping in 3 John 9-10. It seems Diotrephes was "gossiping maliciously" about John and his co-workers. John said Diotrephes "loves to be first." Likewise, gossipers feel important and needed when they can transfer new or scandalous information.

Although some people may classify it as relatively harmless, gossip is placed beside murder, sexual impurity and God-hating in Romans 1:29-32. A man can be disqualified from serving as a deacon if his wife is a gossip (1 Timothy 3:11). Younger widows were advised to remarry so they would not go from house to house and become gossips and busybodies (5:13). Gossiping is serious business.

Stopping the Spread

How can we overcome gossip? When you hear a story, examine your heart. Would you want someone to say the same things about you? Would the Lord be pleased with the story?

Support evidence with the truth. Don't accept hearsay. Ask, "May I quote you?" Many sources shrink back when they have to stand behind their words. Commit yourself to recognizing gossip in its many forms. Then avoid it like the plague.

Flirting With Trouble

Flirtation, flattery, suggestive jesting – these careless words and actions can be like dry tender ready to ignite. Some people humorously flirt, never intending for anything immoral to come of it. But given certain circumstances – perhaps a couple's being alone, a person's struggling with low self-esteem, or someone's enduring an unhappy marriage – and flirting may evolve into something more. How many full-fledged affairs have flowered from the initial seeds of flirting? Christian men and women need to guard their tongues and their ears against flattery, which may be more than it seems.

Colorblind Words

How colorblind are your words? Careless words also take the form of ethnic joking and stereotypical language.

We all have varying degrees of colorblindness. We accept different skin colors and cultures according to our backgrounds and preconceived ideas. We probably never would be unkind to a person to her face, but we might stereotype her culture or joke about her different ethnic group behind his back.

If we determine to cut out jokes that might hurt someone's feelings, it might banish a lot of jokes. But better fewer jokes than fewer friends because our joke found its mark where it hurts. We should avoid stereotypes by refusing to reference ethnic groups by nicknames or by certain parts of town.

How Are Your Words Exchanged?

Careless words are a lot like the exchange of counterfeit money. When they are put into circulation, they are difficult to track down. They usually are inflated and accumulate much interest. Unfortunately, they are counterfeit and, although often accepted at face value, they can lead to easy speculation.

When we exchange words, remember: We don't have to tell everything we know or say everything we think. As the wise man said in Ecclesiastes 10:12-14, "Words from a wise man's mouth are gracious, but a fool is consumed by his own lips. At the beginning his words are folly; at the end they are wicked madness – and the fool multiplies words."

Fool's Math

Some folks have to ADD a word
To put in their two cents.
Others like to TAKE AWAY,
For words they like to mince.
Some folks count on DIVISION
To leave people in a huff.
But true fools MULTIPLY their words;
They can never say enough!

Think About It

1. Why was Jephthah chosen by the elders to lead Israel against their enemies?

2. What unwise oaths were made by Joshua (Joshua 9) and Saul (1 Samuel 14:24-45)?

3. How are our words irreversible?

4. Why can it boost one's ego to spread and listen to gossip?

5. What did God command in Leviticus 19:16?

6. How can seemingly innocent flirting become dangerous if it goes unchecked?

7. Why do you think Jesus put such importance on the control of careless words in Matthew 12:36-37?

8. Do you agree with this statement: "Four things come not back: the spoken word, the sped arrow, time past, the neglected opportunity"?

9. Why is it important for leaders in the church to have discreet wives?

10. Why can ethnic jokes and cultural stereotypes be so damaging?

Tasteful Words: A Dash of Salt

"The first ingredient in conversation is truth; the next, good sense; the third, good humor; and the fourth, wit"
(Sir William Temple).

*Y*ears ago, salt had the tendency to clump when the air was humid. But after additives were put in, salt could be shaken in any weather. One brand's saltbox illustration of a little girl with salt pouring out under her umbrella immortalizes the fact as well as the slogan, "When it rains, it pours." Then salt could be mixed and blended in any amount, whether just a dash or more was needed.

Likewise, our words need just the right amount of salt to be pleasing to God. Perhaps it is just a dash of salt, an insight of wisdom, to make our speech tasteful and delicious. Whatever the amount, we need the well-blended flavor that only God's wisdom can give. In the next six chapters, some positive qualities of speech that is seasoned with salt will be discussed.

❧ Food ❧
For Thought

"A genuine word of kindness is often the best
lever to raise a depressed spirit to its natural level."

(Arthur Helps)

"More people die of broken hearts
than of swelled heads."

(Charles Hodge)

"Gentle words fall lightly, but they have great weight."

(Unknown)

"Everyone who has ever done a kind deed for us,
or spoken one word of encouragement to us
has entered into the makeup of our character and
of our thoughts, as well as our success."

(George Adams)

"Listening empathetically and carefully selecting
the right words to influence another person
in a more positive, constructive and godly direction
are crucial aspects of encouragement."

(Aubrey Johnson)

Feed on God's Word

Look up these scriptures, and put in
your own words what they mean.

Proverbs 12:18

_____
_____
_____

Proverbs 12:25

_____
_____
_____

Proverbs 16:24

_____
_____
_____

Ecclesiastes 4:9-10

_____
_____
_____

Ephesians 4:29

_____
_____
_____

Encouraging Words:
Always Sunny Side Up?

"But my mouth would encourage you;
comfort from my lips would bring you relief"
(Job 16:5).

S ome people insist on eating the same breakfast food every morning. To them, it doesn't matter that an egg can be prepared many
ways – as an omelet, boiled, poached, scrambled, baked or raw. To
please the palates of certain single-minded folks, the egg must always
be sunny side up.

In the same way, a continual sunny-side-up mindset is held by some
Christians. No matter how they feel inside, they think they always must
encourage other people with a candied, sweet word and a plastic, smil-
ing countenance. They reason that God expects no less. They have a
sort of God-didn't-make-no-frowny-faces complex.

A widow was going through the painful process of choosing a
gravestone for her husband's grave. With no feelings for the woman
or the occasion, the saleswoman blurted, "You lucky lady! During
this month, we have a special on marble gravestones." The wise man
voiced our reaction to this insensitivity: "Like one who takes away a
garment on a cold day, or like vinegar poured on soda, is one who sings
songs to a heavy heart" (Proverbs 25:20).

Certainly joy is a definite attribute of a healthy Christian life, but offering smiles and cheerful words is not the only way to encourage other people. Sometimes a person needs comforting words or perhaps no words at all. Finding the right words to encourage someone isn't always easy. Barnabas was one who seemed to be skilled in this art.

The Encourager

When the church was hesitant to accept a new Christian who had once persecuted their number, a certain man was the first to speak up for him. When the gospel spread to the Greeks, the church sent this man to strengthen and exhort the new brethren. And when a fellow Christian had forsaken the missionary group, this man was willing to defend him and give him another chance.

Who was he? His name was Joseph, but the apostles affectionately called him Barnabas, meaning "Son of Encouragement" (Acts 4:36). Note how Barnabas is described: "When he arrived and saw the evidence of the grace of God, he was glad and encouraged them all to remain true to the Lord with all their hearts. He was a good man, full of the Holy Spirit and faith, and a great number of people were brought to the Lord" (11:23-24). What were the results of his encouragement? Many people became Christians.

What about us? Could the church compliment each of us with the nickname "The Encourager"?

Gone to the Dogs?

Encouraging words don't come naturally for us humans. Without thinking, we find it easy to deprecate and discourage. Parents sometimes unconsciously entrench patterns of low self-esteem in their children by criticizing them constantly instead of affirming them. Yet Kenneth Erickson reported that a mother dog gives her young pups nine gentlings for every nip or growl. Sometimes man seems less humane than his best friend.

Conscious effort is required to say the right thing, and we sometimes fail even when we put forth that effort. Two brothers learned this when one went on vacation and promised to call home every night. The first night he called home and was informed about their beloved cat's death. The vacationing brother was stunned. When he recovered, he told his brother he should have broken the news more gently. "Tonight you should have told me the cat is on the roof. Tomorrow you could have said he fell off so you took him to the vet. The next night you could have said that the cat died."

"Okay, I'll do better," his brother replied.

The next night the vacationing brother called home and asked how everyone was.

"Mom's on the roof," his brother replied.

Walking Alongside

As much as we might try, we can't always be on the giving side of encouraging. At some point we must fill our own reserves of strength, or they will run dry. David, who was a tower of strength to his 400 followers, found himself being threatened with mutiny and death by those same men. Their homes had been ravaged, and their wives had been taken by the Amalekites. They blamed David for their predicament. When he could turn to no other, "David encouraged himself in the LORD his God" (1 Samuel 30:6 KJV). Turning to God is the first step we should take in casting off discouragement. Telling God everything can give us a great sense of release and relief. "Cast all your anxiety on him because he cares for you" (1 Peter 5:7).

Paul explained that if we rely on God, then other people can rely on us: "Praise be to the God and Father of our Lord Jesus Christ, the Father of compassion and the God of all comfort, who comforts us in all our troubles, so that we can comfort those in any trouble with the comfort we ourselves have received from God. For just as the sufferings of Christ flow over into our lives, so also through Christ our comfort overflows" (2 Corinthians 1:3-5).

Earl Palmer described the idea of the word "comfort" in this passage as someone walking alongside someone else so he doesn't have to journey the rest of the way alone. We could say that God walks alongside us in our troubles so we can walk alongside other people when they are distressed.

Encourage One Another Daily

Because every situation is different, we cannot learn a standard set of phrases that will encourage other people all the time. But we can look at general guidelines of ways our words can affirm people who need encouragement.

Whatever the situation, we should be hesitant to say, "I understand how you feel." Even if circumstances are similar, it would be extremely difficult to know exactly how another person is feeling. Even if we do understand, the person might not think we do. Perhaps it is wiser to say, "I care about you."

Sickness. The ill do not need long-winded tirades, accounts of relatives' deaths from a similar disease or an in-depth interrogation about their illness. Rather a quiet, short, cheerful visit is usually welcome. A prayer would be appropriate.

Depression. Everyone has felt the pangs of depression. In fact, it is one of the most common mental health disorders in the United States. Depression can take on many guises, including physical illness, hyperactivity, eating disorders, drug abuse and withdrawal. We need to look beyond the symptoms and try to understand the causes of the despair.

Pat answers and stern judgments will not console the discouraged person just as a bandage placed over a festering wound does little good; first the wound must be cleansed of its infection. The same goes for the downtrodden heart. Allowing a person the chance to talk and providing an emotional release valve for the turmoil inside can prove helpful. Cliche solutions such as "Don't worry," "Everything will be all right," or "Relax … take it easy" won't help.

Often we say nothing to someone who is discouraged because we don't know what to say. But our silence might cause the person to wonder if anyone cares at all. In *Those Who Wait*, Rosemary McKnight offers some specific apples of gold, apt words that might encourage someone who is having problems. The statement "I'm sorry you are having problems" expresses concern and acknowledges the fact without judging. Other helpful comments might include "Remember, I love you"; "I am thinking of you"; "I hope this week is a good one for you"; and "You are in my prayers."

Sorrow. The finality or shock of the death of a loved one makes it difficult for words to come to people who have experienced a loss. The grieving often are operating on automatic pilot. Sometimes a friend's just being there in caring silence is what they need. Other people feel a need to talk their feelings out, a process called "obsessive reminiscence." At this time, they don't need Pollyanna phrases such as "It's all for the best," "You have a lot to live for," or "Time heals all." The statement "Death comes to us all" is true, but it ignores the feelings of the bereaved. The more helpful "What can I do to help?" acknowledges the needs of the grieving without interpreting the situation.

The stages of grief can include shock, denial, depression, anger and finally acceptance. Each stage has no prescribed time limit and will be different for each person. Often, people have a time's up attitude for the grieving: "Now it's time for you to get out." Actually, it might not be time at all. The sorrowing need specific offers of help – such as baby-sitting for their kids, helping with the house, or inviting them to dinner – not only right after the funeral but also months later.

Joy. To whom do we first run to tell our good news? We go to someone who can rejoice with us. Ironically, sometimes we find it easier to comfort the troubled than to rejoice with the happy. Paul considered one to be as important as the other: "Rejoice with those who rejoice; mourn with those who mourn" (Romans 12:15). Pride and jealousy are apt to rear their ugly heads unless love prevails. A genuine friend can look beyond herself and truly be happy when good comes to someone else.

Into Your Skin

When people sense that we really care, they are more likely to trust us with their feelings. We need to develop the skill of listening beneath the words. By setting aside our judgments and expectations, we can be of more help. We must feel not only for people but with them. To be true encouragers, we must have the ability to empathize, to get into the skin of another, to understand what she is enduring, hoping or feeling.

In speaking about this empathy, Martin Barbaum said, "Henceforth there shall be such a oneness that when one weeps the other will taste salt." May we seek to have that oneness so that we can truly encourage others with our words.

Think About It

1. Why do you think Paul considered encouraging a gift along with such gifts as serving, teaching and contributing (Romans 12:6-8)?

2. Explain the balance in correcting, rebuking and encouraging that a preacher of the Word should demonstrate (2 Timothy 4:2).

3. How does meeting together serve to encourage one another (Hebrews 10:25)?

4. "Encouragement occurs most effectively when opportunities are seized rather than created" (Lawrence J. Crabb and Dan B. Allender). Give examples of seizing opportunities to encourage.

5. Why does it help grieving or depressed people to talk out their feelings?

6. What are the usual stages of grief? How long do they last?

7. Why is it sometimes difficult to rejoice when other people are rejoicing?

8. What does the name "Barnabas" mean? In what specific instances do we read about his encouraging other people?

9. What are some reasons parents might be overcritical of their children instead of being encouraging?

10. Explain the term "eternal encouragement" Paul wrote about in 2 Thessalonians 2:16-17.

Food For Thought

"Confession is the first step to repentance."
(English proverb)

"Repentance is not only confessing, 'I'm sorry.'
It is also saying, 'I'm through.'"
(Unknown)

"Many blush to confess their faults,
who never blush to commit them."
(William Secker)

"When you pour your heart out, it feels lighter."
(Jewish proverb)

Feed on God's Word

Look up these scriptures, and put in
your own words what they mean.

Psalm 32:1-7

_____
_____
_____

Psalm 103:8-13

_____
_____
_____

Joel 2:2-12

_____
_____
_____

Romans 10:9-10

_____
_____
_____

Philippians 2:10-11

_____
_____
_____

Confessing Words: Acknowledging a Flop or a Favorite

"He who conceals his sins does not prosper,
but whoever confesses and renounces them finds mercy"
(Proverbs 28:13).

*I*t has happened to all of us: We have made the never-fail recipe that somehow fails. The dish of our dreams is transformed into a nightmare. Whether the temperature or the ingredients or the cook's judgment was to blame, we have a flop on our hands. We are faced with the choice of grinning and eating it or dashing to the store for a quick substitute. We might find it difficult to acknowledge our blunder, especially if the occasion is important.

On another occasion, however, nothing perks us up more than someone asking, "Who made this?" When someone wants to give us credit for a delicious dish we have toiled over, we are happy to acknowledge the compliment.

Our eagerness to acknowledge the good can be quite different from our desire to admit the bad. The same is true of spiritual acknowledgment or confession. We might be happy to profess our Savior but reluctant to confess our wrongs. Graciously, God has provided ways in which we can do both and be pleasing to Him.

Confessing the Lord

To clear the confusion about his identity, John the Baptist freely confessed that he wasn't the Christ. John made it clear that he was not the Messiah but was the forerunner of the Lamb of God who was promised. He affirmed Jesus and his own position in God's plan (Luke 3:1-18).

Christ Himself made the good confession. During His trial the council was losing its case because of conflicting accounts from false witnesses. They tried to ensnare the Lord in His words, but He kept silent during most of the proceedings. However, when they asked Him if He was the Christ, He answered simply but profoundly that He was. This gave the Jews their alleged claim of blasphemy, and they believed they had a case (Mark 14:53-64).

In 1 Timothy 6:12-13, we have some insight into a Christian's good confession. The word "good" is also translated "beautiful" or "noble." This confession will always be considered beautiful, but it was especially so in that time of persecution when such a confession might cost one her life. Timothy's acknowledgment of his Lord was made "in the presence of many witnesses." This must have been a public confession, much like when a person is baptized today. Although it is not a creedal statement, many repeat the words of the eunuch in Acts 8:37: "I believe that Jesus Christ is the Son of God."

Jesus spoke about the importance of our confessing Him in Matthew 10:32-33: "Whoever acknowledges me before men, I will also acknowledge him before my Father in heaven. But whoever disowns me before men, I will disown him before my Father in heaven." Soon after these comments were made, His believers were tested. The Jews had ordered that anyone who professed Jesus was the Christ was to be put out of the synagogue (John 9:22). The mildest form of this dreaded punishment consisted of being cut off from friends, family and all religious privileges for 30 days. If the Jew did not repent of his offense, a more severe sentence was pronounced. After the church was established, expulsion of confessors of Christ was a fixed rule in synagogues.

Later, when harsh persecution rose against the early church, Christians were given a choice – to confess their Lord and die an agonizing death or to deny Him and live. Many Christians chose death. Other people faltered because their faith was not strong enough.

What would we have done if we had lived then? More important, how do we react now when the dangerous consequences of confessing are not so imminent? Are we ashamed to own our Lord? One thing is certain: The persecution of this world cannot dim the glory of the Lord's acknowledging us if we are faithful (Romans 8:16-17).

Now we can make the choice whether we confess or deny our Lord. But a time will come when that decision will be made for us: "At the name of Jesus every knee should bow, in heaven and on earth and under the earth, and every tongue confess that Jesus Christ is Lord, to the glory of God the Father" (Philippians 2:10-11).

Confession of Sins

When we begin a new life through belief, repentance, confession and baptism, we as Christians have a new access to God. What once was un-obtainable – continual forgiveness of our sins – now is available through Christ's blood. "If we confess our sins, he is faithful and just and will forgive us our sins and purify us from all unrighteousness" (1 John 1:9). The guilt-relieving process of confession and forgiveness is one of the great privileges of being a child of God.

Confession of sins has always been important in man's relationship to God. In the Jewish religion, confession plays a prominent role. The early church was urged to "confess your sins to each other and pray for each other so that you may be healed" (James 5:16). Simon the Sorcerer, at-tempting to buy the gift of the Holy Spirit, admitted his greed and asked Peter to pray for him (Acts 8:24).

During the second century, as the church grew and departed from biblical example, the act of confessing was taken to extremes. Public confession of all sins began to be practiced. The rite became more like a court trial than a religious act. After being judged by a priest, a sinner was commanded to perform harsh public acts of penance, which could require years of fasting and prayer. Such penances included wearing only woolen garments, having three haircuts a year, and journeying on religious pilgrimages bound in chains until the chains wore off. The sinner was granted absolution or final forgiveness when penance was completed. Often the penitent's way of life was so altered by fasts, poverty and chastity that he joined monastic societies of monks and nuns who voluntarily chose to undergo those rigors. When confession became so stringent, some church members avoided it entirely until they were on their deathbeds.

After the sixth century the idea of private confession, which began with the Irish Catholics to their soul friends, or priests, spread throughout the Catholic Church. This totally private interview became intensive as the priest began to delve into the motives behind the sins and assign penances accordingly. In 1216 the Lateran Council made auricular confession mandatory for all adult Catholics.

By understanding the abuses and extremes of the past, we can avoid them in the future. God does not require public confession of all sins because we would be confessing or listening to confessions almost all the time for the rest of our lives. We are never required to tell a priest or any other individual every sin we commit, for only God can forgive sins. Graciously, God will forgive and Christ will intercede. Only They need know all our sins.

A Biblical Example

In Acts 19:18-20 we have a graphic example of public confession and accompanying repentance of the Jews and Greeks living in Ephesus: "Many of those who believed now came and openly confessed their evil deeds. A number who had practiced sorcery brought their scrolls together and burned them publicly. When they calculated the value of the scrolls, the total came to fifty thousand drachmas. In this way the word of the Lord spread widely and grew in power."

To demonstrate their sincerity, these Ephesians burned the scrolls on which much of their sorcery was based. The cost of the scrolls proved they were serious. Their actions had a positive effect on the whole church.

Public confession should be like this today. This doesn't mean that a reforming drunk should burn his bottles in a bonfire ceremony – although that might not be a bad idea. The principle here is that the whole community knew the profession of these sorcerers, and only a public demonstration would let everyone know about their change of heart. The outcome of their faith and confession was encouragement and growth for the church. When other people are aware of a problem, confession before the ones who are affected or involved makes them aware of a person's willingness to change, and prayers can be offered on their behalf.

What about confession of private sins – the evil thoughts and actions that only God knows? Does our dirty laundry need to be aired before another Christian or the entire congregation in order for us to receive forgiveness? If only God knows our sin, then He is perhaps the only one who needs to hear our confession. But in cases where sin, although committed privately, involves other people, they should be able to see one's repentance in action.

After David committed adultery with Bathsheba, he wrote the confession of his sin in Psalm 51. He acknowledged before God, "Against you, you only, have I sinned and done what is evil in your sight" (v. 4). The same is true with us. Ultimately, whether our sins are public or private, it is against God that we sin; therefore, we first confess to Him.

How thankful we should be that we have such a merciful, forgiving Lord to whom we can confess and such an omnipotent God whom we can acknowledge!

Think About It

1. Why didn't many of the religious leaders who believed in Jesus confess their faith (John 12:42-43)?

2. Besides confessing sin, what other restitution did the Law of Moses require an Israelite to make if he had wronged someone (Numbers 5:5-8)?

3. In 2 Corinthians 9:13, what did Paul say accompanied the Corinthians' confession of the gospel of Christ?

4. Explain how Ezra and the Israelites confessed and made restitution for the sin of marrying foreign women (Ezra 10).

5. What attitude did King David have about his sin of counting the fighting men (2 Samuel 24:10, 17)?

6. Define "confession" and explain the difference between the two kinds of confession described in the Scriptures.

7. Explain how confession of sins changed by the second century as men departed from the truth.

Food
For Thought

"The words we say will teach if we practice
what we preach."

(Unknown)

"Talk to the Lord about sinners, then talk
to sinners about the Lord."

(Unknown)

"We talk of the Second Coming;
half the world has never heard of the first."

(Oswald J. Smith)

"Many Bible classes today need less 'I think ...'
and more of 'The Bible says ...' in their discussions."

(Rosemary McKnight)

"It is also our responsibility to lead women to Christ
through studying the Word with them."

(Pamela Stewart)

Feed on God's Word

Look up these scriptures, and put in
your own words what they mean.

Proverbs 11:30

_____
_____
_____

Proverbs 13:14

_____
_____
_____

Proverbs 15:7

_____
_____
_____

Proverbs 16:21, 23

_____
_____
_____

Ephesians 4:11-15

_____
_____
_____

Teaching Words:
Sharing Something Good

"I pray that you may be active in sharing your faith,
so that you will have a full understanding of every good thing
we have in Christ" (Philemon 6).

*H*ave you ever noticed how people react when you ask for their recipes? Some cooks act as if they didn't hear you, or perhaps they smile without comment. Other cooks exclaim, "I'm sorry; that recipe has been in my family for 100 years and I can't give it out." It's as if the family has some divine, inherent right to that particular recipe, when perhaps they actually got it off the Internet.

Other cooks gladly part with each intricate detail of a fine dish. It doesn't seem to matter to them that other people will probably share the recipe with more friends who will tell other folks – all of whom will enjoy a tasty treat. These free-hearted souls are just happy to share something good.

Unfortunately, many Christians have attitudes like the it's-fine-but-all-mine cooks. As children of God, they have the recipe of salvation but are unwilling to make it more available for the lost to find. Thankfully, God's plan is not locked away but is free to all who will use and follow it. But what a blessing it would be if all Christians would share the good news of Jesus wholeheartedly.

Passing It On

Throughout the New Testament we see examples of believers who shared the good news about Jesus with other people by their words and lives. This is especially evident in Priscilla and Aquila, Jews who were forced to leave Rome because of Claudius' persecution (Acts 18:2). We don't know when they learned the truth; maybe it was in Rome or later as they worked as tentmakers with Paul in Corinth. But we do know they shared a fuller understanding about baptism with Apollos, who was teaching John's baptism (vv. 25-26).

Notice how Priscilla and Aquila taught their mistaken friend. They didn't smugly keep the truth to themselves. They didn't embarrass Apollos by exposing him publicly. Rather, they taught him in the hospitality and privacy of their home "and explained to him the way of God more adequately" (Acts 18:26). When he gained a better understanding, Apollos was eager to go to Achaia to share the gospel.

Priscilla and Aquila were willing to share with Apollos, who then was ready to share with other people. They did exactly what Paul told Timothy to do: "And the things you have heard me say in the presence of many witnesses entrust to reliable men who will also be qualified to teach others" (2 Timothy 2:2).

How can we continue to share God's message today? We can let our homes serve as places in which we can introduce Christ. Inviting our non-Christian friends to Christian events and introducing them to our Christian friends might be a means to influence them. We can look for opportunities daily to reach people in an effective and natural way. When our words are reinforced by our lives through all these avenues, we have a greater chance to share something good.

Tips From the Teaching Text

In Titus 2, the "teaching text" of the Bible, Paul offered suggestions of ways to appeal to various groups by focusing on their needs. Although offered about 2,000 years ago, his suggestions remain timeless.

Teach what is true. "You must teach what is in accord with sound doctrine" (Titus 2:1). Paul told Timothy to ground himself in the Word and to handle it correctly (2 Timothy 2:15). The apostle later warned Timothy to be prepared because men would not insist on sound doctrine but turn aside to myths. The same can happen today if we are not conscientiously striving to stick with God's truth.

Paul had warned earlier: "If anyone teaches false doctrines and does not agree to the sound instruction of our Lord Jesus Christ and to godly teaching, he is conceited and understands nothing. He has an unhealthy interest in controversies and quarrels about words that result in envy, strife, malicious talk, evil suspicions and constant friction between men of corrupt mind, who have been robbed of the truth and who think that godliness is a means to financial gain" (1 Timothy 6:3-5).

Teach with the right attitude and speech. "In your teaching show integrity, seriousness and soundness of speech that cannot be condemned, so that those who oppose you may be ashamed because they have nothing bad to say about us" (Titus 2:7-8). We must not give anyone cause to question our sincerity as a Christian.

Teach "where they are." In Titus 2, Paul told Titus what each different group (older men, older women, younger women, younger men, slaves) should be taught. Every person has her own background and circumstances in life that make her what she is. For that reason, each person should be taught with her needs and learning styles in mind.

In teaching the Ethiopian eunuch, Philip "began with that very passage of Scripture and told him the good news about Jesus" (Acts 8:35). In the same way, we need to care about people enough to learn where they are spiritually and begin at that point. To help believers understand how to reach the lost, Thom Rainer surveyed attitudes of people not affiliated with any church in his book *The Unchurched Next Door*. He designed a scale of five faith stages ranging from those highly resistant to those highly receptive to the gospel. His research uncovered a surprising conclusion: Most unchurched people would welcome an invitation to worship services. We just need to ask.

Put your teaching into practice. "In everything set them an example by doing what is good" (Titus 2:7). Paul told slaves, the lowest rung on society's ladder, how they could make the gospel message appealing to the richest and most influential people in the world at that time. By pleasing their masters and not stealing or talking back to them, they could make "the teaching about God our Savior attractive" (v. 10). Their good lives could draw other people to Christ.

Haddon W. Robinson, quoted in Joseph C. Aldrich's *Life-Style Evangelism*, stated:

> Outsiders to faith are first drawn to Christians and then to Christ. Unfortunately, not all Christians attract. Like a turned magnet, some repel. Yet Christians, alive to God, loving, caring, laughing, sharing, involved at the point of people's need, present an undeniable witness for Christ in their society (p. 11).

The verbal message of the good news without the beauty of a pure life loses much of its impact. Our words must be reinforced by the statement of our lives.

People who possess God in their hearts will want to express it. For too long we have thought our godly presence was all that other people needed in order to see Christ and come to Him. But as Aldrich stated,

> Presence alone is not enough. No one is good enough to just let his life speak for Christ. Words (proclamation) are necessary to point beyond himself to Christ. Nevertheless, the unbeliever needs to feel the impact of the gospel (good news that Christ loves people), and not merely listen to it. When love is felt the message is heard. But presence which never leads to proclamation is an extreme to be avoided. We are "fishers of men," sent to catch fish, not frogmen who dive under water and swim with the fish, making our "presence" known. A healthy presence increases the impact of the gospel's proclamation because it helps predispose people to perceiving the gospel as good news (p. 83).

He's Counting on Us

A story is told about what could have happened when Jesus returned to heaven after His time spent on earth. As He was welcomed by the heavenly host, Gabriel greeted Him and asked about His time on earth.

"Do they all know how much You love them and suffered for them?" Gabriel questioned.

"No, I've left the job for a few good friends of Mine who will tell others. Eventually, the whole world will know about My love and mercy," Jesus answered.

Gabriel was skeptical. "But what if they or the ones after them lose heart and quit? Do You have alternate plans?"

Our Lord said, "No, I'm counting on them."

He is counting on us. God could have chosen any number of ways to spread the good news. He could have showered the world with "God Loves You" bumper stickers, or He could have sent planes trailing banners with John 3:16. Instead He chose us to communicate the message.

One of Christ's last commands on earth was to teach. With that charge He gave the apostles, as well as us, the great responsibility and privilege of spreading His good news. Are we fulfilling the command? How appealing is the gospel according to us? Are we sharing something good – or rather the best thing we've ever known?

Think About It

1. Why should a teacher use different teaching techniques to reach his or her students?

2. According to 2 Timothy 2:23-26, with what attitude should Christians instruct other people?

3. Why weren't the Hebrew brethren ready to be teachers (Hebrews 5:11-14)?

4. Why is our godly presence alone not enough to reach people for Christ?

5. How does Romans 10:14-15 stress the importance of the role of teachers?

6. What instructions are given in 2 John 7-11 about how to treat deceivers who do not continue in the teaching of Christ?

7. How do troublemakers use their words to cause division among people who follow Christ's teaching (Romans 16:17-19)?

8. How did Andrew, Ananias, Philip, Peter, Paul and Silas share the good news?

9. How did Priscilla and Aquila share the truth with Apollos?

10. What did Paul say must be done to the deceivers in Titus 1:10-16?

 Food For Thought

"Praise God even when you
don't understand what He is doing."

(Henry Jacobsen)

"As the Greek said, many men know
how to flatter; few know how to praise."

(Wendell Phillips)

"If gratitude is due from children to their
earthly parent, how much more is gratitude of the
great family of men due to our Father in heaven."

(Hosea Ballou)

"God's Word tells us of His love;
our words should tell Him of our love."

(Unknown)

"The sweetest of all sounds is praise."

(Xenophon)

Feed on God's Word

Look up these scriptures, and put in
your own words what they mean.

Psalm 34:1

_____
_____
_____

Psalm 40:3

_____
_____
_____

Psalm 71:14-15

_____
_____
_____

Psalm 89:1

_____
_____
_____

Romans 15:5-6

_____
_____
_____

Praising Words:
Praising the Creator of an Original Recipe

"Through Jesus, therefore, let us continually offer to God a
sacrifice of praise – the fruit of lips that confess his name"
(Hebrews 13:15).

I am one of those cook-by-the-book cooks. I go by the letter of the
recipe. If it calls for ⅛ teaspoon, I scramble until I find the correct
utensil. I'm a slave to measurement, and I clutch my well-worn recipe
card like a security blanket.

I have the greatest admiration for someone who has the courage to
experiment and create a new dish from scratch. What confidence it
must take to boldly face the culinary unknown. To pour, mix, dash and
pinch ingredients together to make an original gourmet delight is a true
achievement. Our cuisine is constantly expanding by someone's brave
efforts, and our taste buds reap the benefits. Although we might not
know who the originator of a dish was, we wish we knew her identity so
we could sing her praises.

The Original Creator

We do know one Creator. He is a Creator in the truest sense. He didn't
take ingredients to make His initial creation; He made something from
nothing. His creation consists not of one creation but of a multitude of
creations, all of which are "very good."

As God's creation, we should acknowledge Him as our Creator. We can honor our Lord in many ways and one of these is praising Him through our words. Praising God is a response to His goodness, a natural expression of adoration and gratitude for what He has done. Man is not always deserving of our praise, but God is. He is deserving of more praise than we could ever give. As Paul Dribble said, "You don't have to be afraid of praising God too much; unlike humans he never gets a big head."

Biblical Examples of Praise

God's people have been praising Him for a long time. In a variety of circumstances and places, they have felt the need to glorify God. What were some of the reasons for their praise?

The beauty of nature. Probably the person most known for his praise to God was the sweet singer, David. Whether he was tending his sheep, fleeing from Saul, or leading his soldiers into battle, David often marveled at the majesty of God's creation in nature. He wrote songs of praise about nature found in the Psalms (19:1-6; 24:1-2; 29; 96:11-13). The book of Psalms is so full of praise that the Hebrew term for psalms can be translated as "praises."

The joy of blessings. On seeing the generous response of the people to furnish the temple, David led praises to God (1 Chronicles 29:20). When Mary, the mother of Jesus, heard Elizabeth's blessing, she cried a song of praise (Luke 1:46-55). After months of silence caused by his unbelief, Zechariah uttered praise to God with his first words after his son, John, was born (v. 64). These blessings were great occasions for joy and praise.

Victory over enemies. Moses and Miriam broke into songs of praise after the Red Sea miraculously parted for them but swallowed their Egyptian enemies (Exodus 15:1-21). Deborah and Barak sang praises after the defeat of Sisera and his armies (Judges 5). When delivered from Saul, David glorified the Lord (2 Samuel 22). Jehoshaphat, jubilant over a victory from the Lord, assembled his army to praise God in the Valley of Beracah or "Valley of Praise" (2 Chronicles 20:26). God prevailed over His enemies and the people were full of praise.

Milestones in life. After seven years of building the temple, Solomon led praises at the dedication ceremony (1 Kings 8:56-61). Centuries later, Hezekiah joined his people in praising God when the temple was rededicated after years of disuse (2 Chronicles 29:30). After returning from Babylonian captivity and rebuilding the temple's foundation, the Jews' shouts of joyful praise blended with the tears of those who remembered the original temple (Ezra 3:11-13). These were all milestones for the Hebrew people. After years of wandering and then defending their land, they had a permanent place to worship God.

Church growth. Praise was an integral part of the early church's activities. Besides meeting together, breaking bread and sharing fellowship meals, they praised God for His revelation of grace. During the reign of Roman Emperor Trajan (A.D. 103-104), the Christians were said to have met before daybreak to praise Christ.

Events beyond understanding. After Job had lost his family, health and possessions, he fell prostrate in worship and said, "Naked I came from my mother's womb, and naked I will depart. The LORD gave and the LORD has taken away; may the name of the LORD be praised" (Job 1:21). David questioned why God had forgotten him but then said, "I trust in your unfailing love … I will sing to the LORD for He has been good to me" (Psalm 13:5-6). Both men did not understand everything that had happened to them, but they trusted their futures to God and praised Him anyway.

Although our circumstances might not be exactly the same, we can find similar reasons to praise God. When we are victorious over temptation and the devil, we can praise God. When we experience milestones in our lives like births, graduations, weddings or promotions, we have more opportunities to praise Him. All the blessings we see in church growth or the beauty of nature give us greater reasons to adore the Father. Even when we don't understand the Lord's working in our lives, we can praise God for the promise that all things will work together for good if we love Him.

Praising the Lord Today

If we are faithful, we will one day be praising God with the angels in heaven. How will we want to spend eternity praising Him if we don't genuinely praise Him now? Let us focus on how we can improve our praise to the Lord.

Meditate on the Psalms. Read them aloud. Sing them as hymns. Note how David and the other writers praised God in many different circumstances.

Pray. Make praise and adoration an important part of your prayer life. Tell God what He means to you. Let some of your prayers consist solely of praise and thanksgiving.

Avoid vain repetitions. Expressions such as "Praise the Lord," "Praise God," or "Hallelujah," can lose their meaning if they are over-used. Make sure that you know what you are saying when you use praise expressions. Giving thanks is serious business and you need to mean what you say.

Sing. "Is anyone happy? Let him sing songs of praise" (James 5:13). Singing is a natural response when we are happy. Don't worry about how you sound. The melody isn't nearly as important as what is in your heart. Make sure that you always participate in the singing during worship, but let your praise in song follow you in other places as well.

Our praise should come from hearts swelling with adoration and love for God's majesty and care. Whether it is for a lovely sunset, the baptism of a friend, a long-awaited answer to prayer, or even for circumstances we do not fully understand, we should in all things give praise to God. He is the source of every good and perfect gift and will not abandon His people. "Praise the Lord. How good it is to sing praises to our God, how pleasant and fitting to praise Him!" (Psalm 147:1).

Think About It

1. Give examples of biblical characters praising God.

2. Why is our Creator worthy of praise?

3. Find specific psalms that David wrote, and tell about the circumstances in which they were written. How was David able to praise God in each circumstance?

4. List some times when Jesus praised His Father in heaven (example: Matthew 11:25; Luke 10:21).

5. Look at songs of praise in your hymnal. What biblical passages inspired them? Note how many come from the Psalms.

6. How can our songs of praise in worship be more effective?

7. What actions in our lives bring praise to God according to Romans 15:7; Philippians 1:9-11; Hebrews 13:15-16; and 1 Peter 4:11?

8. What are some of the blessings Paul praised God for in 2 Corinthians 1:3-4 and Ephesians 1:3?

9. What items could you include in a prayer of praise and thanksgiving?

10. What should we do if we suffer as a Christian (1 Peter 4:16)?

Food For Thought

"Instead of complaining because
you don't get what you want, be thankful you
don't get what you deserve."

(Unknown)

"Gratitude is born in hearts
that take time to count up past mercies."

(Charles E. Jefferson)

"Who does not thank
for little will not thank for much."

(Estonian proverb)

"Do not take anything for granted —
not one smile or one person or one rainbow or
one breath, or one night in your cozy bed."

(Terri Guillemets)

"God gave you a gift of 86,400 seconds today.
Have you used one to say 'thank you'?"

(William A. Ward)

Feed on God's Word

Look up these scriptures, and put in
your own words what they mean.

Psalm 30:12

_____
_____
_____

Proverbs 27:21

_____
_____
_____

2 Corinthians 9:11

_____
_____
_____

Colossians 2:6-7

_____
_____
_____

1 Timothy 2:1-2

_____
_____
_____

Appreciative Words: Sampling a Rare Treat

"He who receives a benefit should never forget it;
he who bestows should never remember it"
(Pierre Charron).

Grocery store shelves are filled with exotic spices and unusual foods that were not always available. Fresh seafood, succulent fruits and tantalizing vegetables can be shipped to American markets in a matter of hours. Dishes that were once rare can be whipped up in minutes.

But while we enjoy so many conveniences in our society, one treat is becoming more rare. That treat is a simple "thank you" or "good job." Appreciation is becoming a rare dish that is served infrequently.

A 90 Percent Forgetful Crew

In Luke 17, we read about a group of men who forgot to say thanks – all except one. That one, otherwise maligned for his nationality, stands as an example of gratitude to us.

Ten men had leprosy, a dreaded, contagious disease that was quarantined by law. Lepers had to stand at least 50 yards away from a healthy person if they were downwind.

Suffering physical isolation, these men were isolated emotionally as well. The lepers themselves yelled, "Unclean, unclean," as they approached uninfected people so healthy folks would be warned and could move away. Lepers were not to touch other people or to be touched. The original "Untouchables" had to live outside the city walls in a colony by themselves. Sharing the same misery provided perhaps some degree of comfort to the lepers. Even a hated Samaritan was accepted by infected Jews. Leprosy knew no discrimination in its ranks.

Out of their physical and emotional misery and deprivation, these lepers sought Jesus, the Great Physician. In healing them, the Lord not only gave them healthy skin but also renewed possibilities for self-esteem, social contact and fellowship. They owed Jesus a great deal. But in giving them so much, He could not make them grateful. Only the Samaritan returned to thank Jesus.

How would we react if we had been one of the lepers healed by Jesus? Would we have remembered to thank Him?

Ten Percent Return?

Do we have as high a percentage of return today? Does one out of 10 people return to say, "Thanks" or "That was good"? Why don't we go to the trouble to show our appreciation? How do we cultivate the attitude of gratitude?

Are we blinded by too many possessions? Our gratitude level often falls as our material wealth increases.

Are we smugly satisfied in our own abilities? The humanistic I-got-me-where-I-am-today philosophy leaves little room for appreciation of God or other people.

Have we selectively lost our memories? We might remember a slight made against us for years but forget a kindness soon afterward. That's like the woman who ran out of gas on a busy city street. Two muscular men offered to push her to the nearest gas station. When they finally arrived, she steered past it. When they asked her why, she exclaimed that she always goes to the gas station down the street because the gas is cheaper.

Have we failed to recognize the giver of all gifts? God is the gracious benefactor of every good and perfect blessing (James 1:17). We owe Him everything we are and have. Some African Christians sing this pidgin refrain, which emphasizes the source of all blessings: "The things where we get em Papa, Now we bring em back to you."

Do we think we don't really have much for which to be thankful?

One visit to a nursing home, rehabilitation clinic or veteran's hospital can squelch that sentiment. We can always find someone in better shape than we are and someone worse.

Paul's Attitude of Gratitude

Paul told the Thessalonians, "Be joyful always; pray continually; give thanks in all circumstances, for this is God's will for you in Christ Jesus" (1 Thessalonians 5:16-18). For Paul, contentment in every situation wasn't an impossible dream but a reachable goal. No matter how tough the situation was – shipwreck, imprisonment, beatings, stonings – Paul strove to keep a thankful spirit. His attitude wasn't just a stoic "grit your teeth and be thankful." He had a firm basis for his feelings. He put it in a nutshell, "But thanks be to God! He gives us the victory through our Lord Jesus Christ" (1 Corinthians 15:57). Paul saw through faith's eyes the ultimate crown for Christians in heaven. His thankfulness was always directed upward.

Paul also wrote that appreciation should be coupled with our requests to God: "Do not be anxious about anything, but in everything, by prayer and petition, with thanksgiving, present your requests to God" (Philippians 4:6). As Dwight Moody paraphrased, "Be careful for nothing, prayerful for everything, thankful for anything."

An ever-thankful spirit was demonstrated by the biblical scholar Matthew Henry. His modest home was burglarized, but the cheerful old gentleman entered in his diary this observation: "Let me be thankful first, because he never robbed me before; second, because although he took my purse, he did not take my life; third, because although he took all I possessed, it was not much; and fourth, because it was I who was robbed, and not I who robbed."

Sending and Accepting Flowers

Often we are hesitant to express our appreciation to people because they might react negatively. They could possibly misunderstand our motives ("What does she really want?") or feel themselves undeserving ("She can't really mean that") or think themselves immodest if they agree ("She will think I'm bragging"). Giving and accepting appreciation can be almost as difficult as giving and receiving criticism.

Corrie ten Boom's unique way of accepting affirmations is described in Kenneth Erickson's book *The Power of Praise*. She said,

> "Every time a person praises me for something I've done, I just accept it as a flower. Then at the end of the day I put all the flowers together into a lovely bouquet, get on my knees, and say, 'Here, Father, this bouquet belongs to You! The lovely things people have said about me, they were really saying about You. Thank You, Father, for using me'" (p. 74).

Why can't we send flowers of gratitude? The extra effort to say "thank you" or "good work" doesn't cost a lot or take much time, but it can make all the difference.

Sadly, the most appreciation some people get is at their funerals. Orators extol the deceased's virtues with flowery adjectives while teary-eyed mourners nod in agreement. What a shame that these words never were said while the person in the casket could have heard them.

Flowers

If lovely flowers to me you give,
Please let me have them while I live.
I cannot see them after death,
Or catch their scent without a breath.
Words of praise that are expressed,
Cannot be heard when I'm at rest.
If any love you have for me,
Please give it now while I can see,
For all the flowers that you lay on
Can't touch my heart when I am gone!
— Unknown

Think About It

1. Why do you think people don't show their gratitude more often?

2. How were lepers emotionally and physically isolated?

3. What are some ways to cultivate the attitude of gratitude?

4. Find scriptures in which Jesus told about the difficulty rich people have in keeping the right attitude toward their possessions (Luke 12:13-21; 18:18-25).

5. Why are we more prone to remember a slight done to us than a kindness?

6. How can one be "always giving thanks to God the Father for everything, in the name of our Lord Jesus Christ" even in tragedy and persecution (Ephesians 5:20)?

7. How is a man "tested by the praise he receives" (Proverbs 27:21)?

8. "People are always too busy to say 'Thanks' but never too busy to serve as pallbearer" (Unknown). Do you agree?

9. Give examples of Jesus' thanking God before eating.

10. What is the "indescribable gift" for which Paul said we should be thankful in 2 Corinthians 9:15?

✥Food✥
For Thought

"The righteous need no tombstones;
their words are their tombstones."

(Talmud)

"Jesus is God spelling Himself out in
language that men can understand."

(S.D. Gordon)

"The single biggest problem in communication
is the illusion that it has taken place."

(George Bernard Shaw)

"The more we elaborate our means
of communication, the less we communicate."

(J.B. Priestley)

"God has stated in clear and concise language
how He created the universe,
and we ought not to doubt His Word."

(Walter Lang)

Feed on God's Word

Look up these scriptures, and put in
your own words what they mean.

Isaiah 53:7, 9

_____
_____
_____

Malachi 2:6

_____
_____
_____

Matthew 13:34-35

_____
_____
_____

Luke 4:22

_____
_____
_____

John 14:23-27

_____
_____
_____

The Finishing Garnish: Learning From the Master

"Simon Peter answered him, 'Lord, to whom shall we go? You have the words of eternal life' "
(John 6:68).

*P*eople who take the culinary arts seriously enroll in a cooking school to learn from a master chef. Among other things, students learn the importance of the appearance of the end product. A professional chef would not permit a dish to be served without a finishing garnish – a lemon wedge, a sprig of parsley, a dollop of whipped cream topped with a cherry. That finishing touch crowns fastidious care and expertise. It separates fine cuisine from fast food. The garnish truly makes a difference.

Likewise, spiritually our lives must be garnished with the touch of the Master. The original meaning of "garnish" was "to equip oneself, prepare, protect, and put in order" (Webster). How can we know if our spiritual lives are equipped and put in order?

The Tongue Test

James wrote about a sure-fire way of telling if a person's life is spiritually garnished: "If anyone considers himself religious and yet does not keep a tight rein on his tongue, he deceives himself and his religion is worthless. ... We all stumble in many ways. If anyone is never at fault in what he says, he is a perfect man, able to keep his whole body in check" (James 1:26; 3:2).

James says that if a person passes the tongue test, he is on his way to true Christian maturity. This isn't an easy test to pass. We can improve our score daily by evaluating our speech on the basis of Colossians 3:17: "And whatever you do, whether in words or deed, do it all in the name of the Lord Jesus, giving thanks to God the Father through him." Are we glorifying God through our speech? Could every word we utter be offered in the name of Jesus?

Our Lord passed the "tongue test" with flying colors. He was tempted to curse, swear, gossip, blaspheme and lie just as we are, yet He resisted each temptation. He spoke words of love and truth, causing even His enemies to acknowledge His power. When the temple guards who had been sent to arrest Jesus returned empty-handed, they declared, "No one ever spoke the way this man does" (John 7:46). The Son of God was the perfect Master of words, and we would do well to emulate Him.

The Communicating Christ

Whether Christ spoke to one person or a crowd of thousands, He touched people with His words. He was able to reach all kinds of individuals in many different circumstances. Here are some of the C's of His winning communication skills.

Concise words. Jesus didn't waste words. His sermons were to the point, not tedious discourses. He answered questions succinctly. He gave direct explanations to His parables. He got full mileage out of His words.

Clear words. Jesus' teachings could be so simple that even a child could understand them. He sometimes elected to veil spiritual principles in the language of parables to separate people yearning to believe from people who were critical of His mission (Matthew 13:11-17). Without difficult or sophisticated meanings, His words were impressive enough.

Concrete words. Sparrows, lilies, houses, sheep, yeast, mustard seeds, coins – these and other touchable objects were used by Jesus to get His message across. The tangible was required to make the intangible lessons about love, worry, forgiveness, preparation and growth come to life.

Convicting words. Christ's words caused His listeners to think, re-examine and often determine to change. Not only did His admonition to sin no more touch the adulteress caught in the act, but His invitation to cast the first stone cut into the consciences of the self-righteous teachers and Pharisees. They had brought the woman to be judged but instead had indicted themselves (John 8:1-11).

Commanding words. The Lord amazed the crowds with His commanding words (Matthew 7:28-29). Unlike the teachers of the Law, Jesus spoke with authority, so much so that the Jewish leaders wished to have no more verbal tangles with Him. In all their trickery, they could not trip up our Lord.

Comforting words. "Do not let your hearts be troubled. Trust in God, trust also in me. ... Peace I leave with you; my peace I give you" (John 14:1, 27). The words that comforted Jesus' first disciples also comfort us. Whether a family mourned the loss of a loved one, a victim of disease longed for relief, or a soul was caught in the clutches of sin, Jesus' soothing words could heal – physically and spiritually. Where can one find more consoling words than these: "Come to me, all you who are weary and burdened, and I will give you rest. Take my yoke upon you and learn from me, for I am gentle and humble in heart, and you will find rest for your souls. For my yoke is easy and my burden is light" (Matthew 11:28-30).

Compassionate words. No matter what He said, Jesus always loved the people with whom He spoke. When He approached Jerusalem for the Passover the last time, He wept over the inhabitants' sinful plight. Even while suffering on the cross, Jesus didn't forget to make provisions for the care of His mother or to forgive His tormentors. He cared.

Clever words. Our Lord was master of clever answers to entangling questions. When the Jewish leaders questioned His authority, He shot a question about John's baptism back to them (Luke 20:1-8). When spies tried to entrap Him concerning paying taxes to Caesar, they were silenced by His wisdom (vv. 20-26). When the Sadducees asked about marriage in the resurrection, Jesus answered so cleverly that the teachers of the Law commended Him in spite of themselves (vv. 27-39).

Confronting words. Some of Jesus' words were so tough that they were hard to swallow. Once when confronted by His "hard teaching," many of His followers deserted Him (John 6:60-66). He was not afraid to confront the scribes and Pharisees for their hypocrisy (Matthew 23).

Jesus overturned the stalls of the irreligious money-changers in the temple and denounced their sinful practice (21:12-13). He loved people, but He didn't shirk from confronting them with their sins when it was necessary.

All these encompassing images give us a fuller portrait of the Son of God. In Him we see the perfect example for living. The Hebrews writer tells us to keep our eyes on Jesus, "the author and finisher of our faith" (Hebrews 12:2 KJV). The original Greek can be translated as the "beginner and completer of faith." Just like the chef must garnish or finish her product, so our faith through Christ can be finished or made complete. As R.C.H. Lenski stated, "From start to finish we need the divine Christ as the one who can fill us with faith, keep us in faith, and finally crown our faith."

Our faith will be crowned only if we have controlled our tongues. We will have to give an account of every careless word we have spoken. It's as if judgment will be the great replay. Every word we speak is being recorded and will be played back to us on judgment. We might want to fast-forward some of the things we have said, but unless those evil words have been erased and forgiven by the blood of Jesus, they will be played exactly as we said them. "What you have said in the dark will be heard in the daylight, and what you have whispered in the ear in the inner rooms will be proclaimed from the roofs" (Luke 12:3). This should make us think before we speak.

Our words should be soft and sweet because we don't know which ones we will have to eat. A preacher, looking for a gimmick to bolster attendance, announced after Sunday morning services that several recorders hidden under the pews would be played back Sunday night. Several offers were made to purchase the recordings before they were played.

Some of our friends who served as missionaries to Germany had a simple ritual before every meal. The folks around the table clasped hands and bowed their heads to thank God for the food. After the prayer was finished, a wish was spoken in German that everyone would find the meal tasty and enjoyable. My wish is the same for you spiritually. May your words be tasteful, "full of grace, seasoned with salt." Guten Appetitt!

Think About It

1. Why do you think James put so much emphasis in his epistle on mastery of the tongue in being a mature Christian?
2. What does it mean to "do all in the name of the Lord" (Colossians 3:17)?
3. Find examples in the Gospels of Jesus' words that were:
   a. Concise
   b. Clear
   c. Concrete
   d. Convicting
   e. Commanding
   f. Comforting
   g. Compassionate
   h. Clever
   i. Confronting

Bibliography

Adams, J. Donald. *The Magic and Mystery of Words.* New York: Holt, Rinehart and Winston, 1963.

Aldrich, Joseph C. *Life-Style Evangelism.* Portland: Multnomah, 1981.

Benjamin, Kathy. "60% of People Can't Go 10 minutes Without Lying." *Mental Floss.* 7 May 2012. <http://mentalfloss.com/article/30609/60-people-cant-go-10-minutes-without-lying>.

Brewer, Ralph E. "It Had a Little Bad Language, But ... ." *Gospel Advocate*, 129 (Dec. 3, 1987) 718-719.

Bumbalough, Debbie and Dwina Willis, eds. *Woman to Woman.* Nashville: Gospel Advocate, 2007.

Caine, Lynn. *Being a Widow.* New York: William Morrow, 1988.

Crabb, Lawrence J. and Dan B. Allender. *Encouragement: The Key to Caring.* Grand Rapids: Zondervan, 1984.

Dobson, James. *Emotions: Can You Trust Them?* Ventura: Regal, 1980.

Dodge, Richard Irving. *The Plains of North America and Their Inhabitants.* Edited by Wayne R. Kine. Newark: Univ. of Delaware Press, 1989.

Donoghue, Quentin and Linda Shapiro. *Bless Me, Father, for I Have Sinned.* New York: Donald I. Fine, 1984.

Erickson, Kenneth. *The Power of Praise.* St. Louis: Concordia, 1984.

Frankforter, A. Daniel. *A History of the Christian Movement.* Chicago: Nelson-Hall, 1978.

Golde, Roger A. *What You Say Is What You Get.* New York: Hawthorn, 1979.

Johnson, Aubrey. *The Barnabas Factor.* Nashville: Gospel Advocate, 2004.

Johnson, B.W. *John.* The New Testament Commentary, Vol. 3. Delight, Ark.: Gospel Light, 1886.

Jones, Richard. "Growing in Praise." *Gospel Advocate*, March 1990, 34.

Kelso, Mrs. Marvin. "Swearing by Any Other Name." *Christian Woman,* Sept./Oct. 1987, 15.

Leman, Kevin. *Making Children Mind Without Losing Yours.* New York: Dell, 1984.

McKnight, Rosemary. *Those Who Wait.* Nashville: Gospel Advocate, 1989.

Pippert, Rebecca Manley. *Out of the Salt Shaker and Into the World.* Downers Grove, Ill.: InterVarsity, 1979.

Rainer, Thom S. *The Unchurched Next Door: Understanding Faith Stages as Keys to Sharing Your Faith.* Grand Rapids: Zondervan, 2003.

Raymond, Joan. "Who Talks More, Men or Women? Your Guess May Likely be Wrong." *Today Health.* 18 July 2014. < http://www.today.com/health/who-talks-more-men-or-women-your-guess-may-likely-1D79944357>.

Scales, Debbie. "I Don't Mean to Gossip, but … ." *Christian Woman,* Sept./Oct. 1987, 16-18.

Shackelford, Don. *A Survey of Church History.* Dallas: Gospel Teachers, 1962.

Swindoll, Charles R. *The Quest for Character.* Portland: Multnomah, 1987.

Vanceburg, Martha and Sylvia W. Silverman. *Family Feelings: Daily Meditations for Healthy Relationships.* New York: Bantam, 1989.

Walters, Richard. *Anger, Yours and Mine and What to Do About It.* Grand Rapids: Zondervan, 1981.

----------. *How to Say Hard Things the Easy Way.* Dallas: Word, 1991.

----------. *Let Go and Be Free.* High Ground Press, 2002.

Watson, Billy J. "Counseling Angry Persons." *Gospel Advocate,* July 1989, 41.

West, Earl Irvin. *The Search for the Ancient Order,* Vol. 1. Nashville: Gospel Advocate, 1986.

Willhite, Shirley. "By Your Words." *Christian Woman,* Sept./Oct. 1987, 13-14.

CPSIA information can be obtained
at www.ICGtesting.com
Printed in the USA
LVOW04s1228311015

460449LV00003B/5/P